◆ THE FLAVORS OF ◆
BON APPÉTIT

· THE FLAVORS OF ·
BON APPÉTIT
· 1998 ·

from the Editors of Bon Appétit

Condé Nast Books ◆ Pantheon
New York

For *Bon Appétit* Magazine

William J. Garry, *Editor-in-Chief*
Laurie Glenn Buckle, *Editor, Bon Appétit Books*
Marcy MacDonald, *Editorial Business Manager*
Carri Marks, *Editorial Production Director*
Sybil Shimazu Neubauer, *Editorial Administrator*
Jordana Ruhland, *Assistant Editor*
Marcia Lewis, *Editorial Support*
Norman Kolpas, *Text*
Amanda Hesser, *Supplemental Text*
Gaylen Ducker Grody, *Research*

For *Condé Nast* Books

Jill Cohen, *President*
Ellen Maria Bruzelius, *Division Vice President*
Lucille Friedman, *Fulfillment Manager*
Tom Downing, *Direct Marketing Manager*
Jill Neal, *Direct Marketing Manager*
Craig Davis, *Direct Marketing Analyst*
Paul DiNardo, *Direct Marketing Assistant*

Produced in association with Patrick Filley Associates, Inc.
Designed by Laura Hammond Hough

Front Jacket: Chocolate-Whiskey Truffle Soufflés with Caramel Sauce (page 198).

Back Jacket: Top: Lobster and Confetti Vegetable Salad (page 102);
Middle: Beef Tenderloin with Salsa Verde (page 46);
Lower Left: Succotash (page 138); Lower Right: Grilled Rosemary-crusted
Pizzas with Sausage, Peppers and Cheese (page 134).

Contents Page: Top: White Bean, Escarole and Bell Pepper Soup(page 26);
Lower Left: Pan-fried Lamb Chops with Garlic (page 67);
Lower Right: Chocolate-Orange Tart with Almond Crust (page 173).

ISBN 0-375-40227-6

Manufactured in the United States of America

FIRST EDITION

2 4 6 8 9 7 5 3 1

Condé Nast Web Address: http://www.epicurious.com

Random House Web Address: http://www.randomhouse.com

·CONTENTS·

·INTRODUCTION·

Page 14

Any magazine becomes, in its own particular way, a document of its times—a permanent record of the way people think, feel and live their lives. This is certainly true of *Bon Appétit*, where we aim, month after month, to reflect how our readers are cooking, eating, dining out and entertaining today.

When month after month adds up to a year, certain trends begin to emerge. Those trends come into even sharper focus when we make our annual selection of the year's best recipes to include here, in *The Flavors of Bon Appétit*.

As you leaf through the pages that follow, one of the first bold impressions they will likely make is that America's love affair with Italian food continues unabated. You'll certainly find no shortage of the kinds of pastas and pizzas we all seem to crave. Examine the contents of this book a little more closely, though, and you'll find fascinating evidence of how our passion for that nation's cooking grows not only stronger but more refined with the passing years. No longer do we unswervingly seek out the generic Italian food we ate in our childhoods. Instead, we journey, at least figuratively, cross-country in search of regional specialties, a trend celebrated in *Bon Appétit's* May 1997 special collector's issue on "The Italian Countryside." Some of the authentic dishes from that issue appear here.

page 154

The same simple, sun-kissed approach to life that makes us adore Italy and its foods is also found in neighboring countries. So, it is no surprise that a rising interest in the cooking of other lands bordering the Mediterranean can be traced through the pages of *Bon Appétit* during 1997. You'll find it in this book too, represented by such recipes as Greece's Classic Saganaki with Olives and Lemon (page 15) and Grilled Game Hen with Moroccan Spices (page 90).

Just as the best recipes of 1997 demonstrate how our devotion to Italy is broadening to embrace the entire Mediterranean, so, too, do they show how our tastes continue to expand in two other areas: Latin America and Asia.

page 107

Where once we favored, almost exclusively, the foods of Mexico and the American Southwest, now our taste for Latin American cooking also stretches to the cuisines of Central and South America and the Caribbean. By way of example, look for such dishes as Cuban-Style Grilled Mojo Chicken with Avocados and Mangoes (page 78) and a Nicaraguan-inspired Grilled Skirt Steak with Cilantro Chimichurri Sauce (page 50). At the same time, our knowledge and appreciation of Southwestern and Mexican food grows more discerning.

As for Asia, many years have passed since our knowledge

page 110

page 182

of its cuisines moved beyond the Cantonese standards that once were synonymous with Chinese food to take in highlights from Szechwan, Hunan, Beijing, Shanghai and other provinces and cities. At the same time, we began to discover the finer points of the Japanese cuisine; and then, our culinary passports were stamped by India, Thailand and, more recently still, Korea and Vietnam. Who, a decade ago, would have thought that recipes like Coconut-Lime Shrimp with Peanut Sauce (page 17), Spicy Singapore Noodles with Beef and Carrots (page 127) or Lamb Tikka with Crispy Onions (page 67) would sound not only so appealing but also so downright familiar?

Of course, familiarity, for avid cooks, often breeds experimentation. When applied at once to ingredients and preparations from many different lands, the result points to yet another trend well evident in the best recipes of the past year: fusion. Look to Roasted Red Curry Chicken with Apple Jus (page 84) and Pineapple-Coconut Tuiles with Mascarpone Cream (page 212) for two examples of such delicious cross-pollination of cuisines.

In our quest for new taste sensations, we haven't only looked abroad this past year. One other significant trend borne out by this book is the rediscovery of good old American food, reinterpreted in fresh and appealing new ways. Recipes like Butternut Squash and Corn Chowder (page 28) and Pear and Raspberry Cobbler with Buttermilk Biscuits (page 180) speak not only to the pride we feel for our heritage but also to our growing confidence as cooks.

That confidence shows, too, in our approach to healthful cooking, as more and more of us come to realize that moderation is infinitely more successful, and sane, than deprivation. Recipes such as Low-Fat Cassoulet with Turkey Sausage (page 88), Peppered Beef Slices with Green Onions and Radishes (page 55) and Brown Sugar Pineapple Brûlée (page 180) put to rest the outdated notion that good food and healthful food are mutually exclusive concepts.

Linked to our increasing interest in healthful eating, and likely benefitting from it, has been the continued growth of farmers' markets that provide city, suburban and rural dwellers alike with the finest, widest selection of produce available. Scan the recipes here and you will find a celebration of seasonal fruits and vegetables, from Romaine and Roasted-Beet Salad (page 152) to Eggplant with Roasted Pepper, Olive and Feta Salad (page 110) to Apricot-Cherry Shortcakes (page 182).

Cooking with the seasons, eating for health, celebrating American foods, exploring new cuisines from around the world—these top trends from the past year cover so much ground that you might think they share little, if any, common ground. But they do. Each reflects a different aspect of the power good food has to soothe us when times get tough; to warm us when the weather turns cold or cool us when the temperature soars; to draw family and friends together over a home-cooked meal. Whatever the trends of any given year, these basic truths endure.

page 59

·STARTERS·

From left to right: Coconut-Lime Shrimp with Peanut Sauce (page 17); Pan-Asian Teriyaki Spare Ribs (page 70); and Eggplant and Watercress Salad with Sesame Seeds (page 153).

Shrimp and Crab Ceviche with Avocado

◆ ◆ ◆

½	pound plum tomatoes, halved, seeded
1	large red bell pepper, halved, seeded
1	large jalapeño chili, halved, seeded
1	medium (about 10 ounces) white onion, peeled, cut into 6 wedges
6	tablespoons fresh lime juice
2	tablespoons fresh orange juice
1	tablespoon ketchup
1	teaspoon prepared white horseradish
½	teaspoon hot pepper sauce (such as Tabasco)
1	pound cooked peeled deveined large shrimp, cut in half lengthwise
½	cup chopped tomato
½	cup chopped fresh cilantro
1	green onion, chopped
1	ripe avocado, halved, pitted, peeled
½	pound crabmeat, drained, picked over

Preheat broiler. Place tomato halves, bell pepper and jalapeño, skin side up, on baking sheet. Place onion on baking sheet. Broil vegetables until slightly blackened, about 5 minutes. Transfer vegeta-

◆ ◆ ◆

While this refreshing seafood appetizer is now made in most of Central and South America, it was born in Peru, and to this day cooks there are acknowledged as the masters of the dish. In a classically prepared ceviche, the always-present citrus juice is used to "cook" and flavor the seafood; in this inventive recipe, the juice is used to flavor already-cooked shellfish.

◆ ◆ ◆

bles to blender. Add lime juice and next 4 ingredients. Blend until almost smooth. Transfer sauce to large bowl. Season to taste with salt and pepper. Refrigerate until cold. *(Can be prepared 1 day ahead. Cover and keep refrigerated.)*

Add shrimp to sauce. Mix in chopped tomato, cilantro and green onion. Cube 1 avocado half. Slice other half. Fold avocado cubes and crab into ceviche. Garnish with avocado slices and serve.

6 SERVINGS

Lox and Melon with Chives and Lemon

◆ ◆ ◆

½   small to medium honeydew melon, peeled, seeded, sliced
4   ounces thinly sliced lox
3   tablespoons chopped fresh chives
8   thin lemon wedges

Divide melon slices among plates. Top melon slices with lox. Sprinkle chives over. Season to taste with pepper. Place 2 lemon wedges on each plate and serve immediately.

4 SERVINGS

◆ ◆ ◆

This simple appetizer is a clever blend of sweet, salty and tangy flavors. It is reminiscent of that Italian classic, prosciutto and melon, but lower in both fat and calories.

◆ ◆ ◆

Walnut, Arugula and Gorgonzola Crostini

◆ ◆ ◆

Butter, room temperature
18 ¼-inch-thick diagonal baguette bread slices

6 tablespoons chopped toasted walnuts
3 ounces Gorgonzola cheese, crumbled
3 tablespoons finely chopped arugula
Arugula leaves

Preheat oven to 400°F. Spread butter over 1 side of each baguette slice. Arrange baguette slices on baking sheet, butter side up. Bake baguette slices until golden, about 12 minutes. Cool.

Reduce oven temperature to 350°F. Mix walnuts, Gorgonzola and chopped arugula in medium bowl. Spoon nut-cheese mixture evenly atop baguette toasts, pressing to adhere. Season with pepper. Bake toasts until cheese melts, about 6 minutes. Cool crostini slightly. Arrange on platter. Garnish with arugula leaves and serve.

6 SERVINGS

Garlic and Anchovy Dip with Vegetables

◆ ◆ ◆

1 cup extra-virgin olive oil
½ cup (1 stick) unsalted butter
8 canned anchovy fillets, chopped
3 garlic cloves, finely chopped
1 red bell pepper, cut into strips
1 yellow bell pepper, cut into strips
10 celery stalks, cut in half crosswise
6 green onions

Heat first 4 ingredients in heavy medium skillet over low heat until butter melts and mixture simmers, about 3 minutes. Season with salt and pepper. Transfer to flameproof bowl. Place over candle or canned heat burner. Serve with vegetables.

4 SERVINGS

◆ ◆ ◆

This warm Italian dip of melted butter, olive oil, anchovies and garlic is called *bagna cauda* or "hot bath." It is usually accompanied by raw vegetables, including peppers and celery.

◆ ◆ ◆

Classic Saganaki with Olives and Lemon

◆ ◆ ◆

1	8-ounce package kasseri cheese* or pecorino Romano, cut into ½-inch-thick rectangular slices
	All purpose flour
3	tablespoons (about) olive oil
½	lemon
1	tablespoon chopped fresh oregano
	Tomato wedges
	Pita wedges
	Kalamata olives

Rinse cheese slices under cold water (do not pat dry). Coat with flour. Heat oil in heavy large skillet over medium-high heat until almost smoking. Add cheese and cook until beginning to brown, about 1 minute per side. Transfer to plates.

Squeeze lemon over cheese; sprinkle with oregano and pepper. Serve cheese with tomatoes, pita and olives.

Kasseri is a firm sheep's-milk cheese, available at Greek markets and many supermarkets.

4 TO 6 SERVINGS

MELTED CHEESE

Nearly every culture that includes cheese in its cuisine has a classic melted cheese dish. Here are some examples.

◆ Saganaki: The word is Greek for "two-handled frying pan," the kind used to make this specialty. Chunks of kasseri or kefalotyri cheese are dredged in flour, fried in olive oil and sprinkled with lemon juice, oregano or parsley and pepper.

◆ Queso Fundido: Literally "melted cheese" in Spanish, *queso fundido* is a Mexican classic. Jack cheese or a mild cheddar is melted in a shallow dish and brought bubbling hot to the table, accompanied with tortillas and a spicy tomato sauce.

◆ Fondue: A time-honored Swiss recipe, fondue is made with Gruyère, Comte, Emmenthal or Appenzeller cheese, which is melted with white wine, garlic and kirsch. Diners dip into the cheese with chunks of bread on long forks.

◆ Mozzarella in Carrozza: This Italian dish is made by sandwiching slabs of mozzarella between slices of bread, soaking in egg and frying.

◆ Delicias de Queso: A typical *tapa*, these little Spanish cheese balls are made of Gouda (or other soft mild cheese), Parmesan, eggs, onion and ham and fried in hot oil.

◆ ◆ ◆

Bell Peppers Filled with Olives, Anchovies and Pine Nuts

◆ ◆ ◆

3	medium-size red bell peppers
3	medium-size yellow bell peppers
2	tablespoons raisins
1	cup fresh breadcrumbs from French bread
¼	cup brine-cured black olives (such as Gaeta or Kalamata), pitted, chopped
3	tablespoons pine nuts, toasted
3	tablespoons chopped fresh basil
3	tablespoons chopped fresh Italian parsley
2	tablespoons drained capers, chopped
2	medium garlic cloves, minced
2	anchovy fillets, minced
½	teaspoon (scant) salt
5	tablespoons olive oil

Lightly oil 13 x 9-inch baking dish. Char peppers over gas flame or in broiler until blackened on all sides but not soft. Wrap in paper bag and let stand 10 minutes. Peel peppers. Cut lengthwise in half. Cut out stems and scrape out seeds. Arrange peppers, cut side up, in single layer in prepared dish.

Preheat oven to 350°F. Place raisins in small bowl. Add enough hot water to cover. Let stand 10 minutes. Drain raisins; chop coarsely. Place in medium bowl. Add breadcrumbs and next 8 ingredients; toss to combine. Season with pepper. Mix in 3 tablespoons oil. Spoon into peppers. Drizzle 2 tablespoons oil over. *(Can be prepared 6 hours ahead. Cover and chill.)* Bake until peppers are heated through but still hold their shape, about 30 minutes. Serve bell peppers hot or at room temperature.

6 SERVINGS

Coconut-Lime Shrimp with Peanut Sauce

♦ ♦ ♦

PEANUT SAUCE

⅓ cup creamy peanut butter (do not use old-fashioned style
    or freshly ground)
¼ cup canned low-salt chicken broth
2 tablespoons canned unsweetened coconut milk*
1 teaspoon fresh lime juice
1 teaspoon soy sauce
1 teaspoon fish sauce (nam pla)*
1 teaspoon hot pepper sauce (such as Tabasco)

SHRIMP

1 cup coarsely chopped fresh basil
½ cup canned unsweetened coconut milk
1½ tablespoons finely chopped garlic
1½ tablespoons fresh lime juice
1 tablespoon minced peeled fresh ginger
2 teaspoons soy sauce
2 teaspoons fish sauce (nam pla)
2 teaspoons golden brown sugar
20 large uncooked shrimp, peeled, deveined

1 cup hickory smoke chips, soaked in water 30 minutes, drained
4 bamboo skewers, soaked in water 30 minutes, drained

FOR PEANUT SAUCE: Puree all ingredients in processor until smooth. *(Can be prepared 1 day ahead. Cover and refrigerate. Bring to room temperature before using.)*

FOR SHRIMP: Blend first 8 ingredients in processor until almost smooth. Transfer marinade to 13 x 9 x 2-inch glass baking dish. Add shrimp and turn to coat. Cover; chill 2 hours, turning occasionally.

Prepare barbecue (medium-high heat). Place smoke chips in 8 x 6-inch foil packet with open top. Set atop coals. Thread 5 shrimp onto each of 4 skewers. Grill until just cooked through, basting with marinade, about 2 minutes per side.

Serve skewered shrimp with peanut sauce.

Both ingredients are available at Asian markets and in the Asian foods section of many supermarkets.

4 SERVINGS

♦ ♦ ♦

This salty, fermented fish sauce called a *nam pla* is a popular ingredient throughout Southeast Asia. Packed with flavor, only a little is needed to enhance both the shrimp and the accompanying peanut sauce.

♦ ♦ ♦

Crab Fritters with Spicy Lime Sauce

◆ ◆ ◆

◆ ◆ ◆

Here's an Asian—and very elegant—spin on the classic American crab cakes. Panko are Japanese breadcrumbs, and they're available at Asian markets and in the Asian foods section of many supermarkets. That's also where you'll find *nam pla*.

◆ ◆ ◆

SAUCE

½ cup fresh lime juice
6 tablespoons fish sauce (nam pla)
¼ cup pure maple syrup
3 jalapeño chilies, seeded, chopped
2 garlic cloves, chopped

FRITTERS

¼ cup mayonnaise
1 tablespoon Dijon mustard
½ teaspoon grated lemon peel
   Dash of hot pepper sauce (such as Tabasco)
8 ounces fresh crabmeat, drained, picked over

2 grapefruits
2 oranges

1½ cups panko (Japanese breadcrumbs)
   Peanut oil (for frying)

2 firm but ripe avocados, halved, pitted, peeled, sliced
2 tablespoons chopped fresh cilantro
2 tablespoons chopped fresh chives

FOR SAUCE: Mix all ingredients in large bowl to blend. Cover and chill at least 1 hour or overnight to develop flavors.

FOR FRITTERS: Mix first 4 ingredients in medium bowl to blend. Mix in crabmeat. Season with salt and pepper. Shape mixture into six 2¼-inch-diameter patties, using ¼ cup for each. Place fritters on baking sheet. Cover and chill 3 hours.

Cut all peel and white pith from grapefruits. Using small sharp knife, cut between membranes to release segments. Repeat with oranges. Chill segments until ready to serve.

Place panko in shallow dish. Coat each fritter with panko, pressing to adhere. Pour oil into heavy large skillet to depth of ½ inch and heat to 350°F. Cook fritters in batches until brown and heated through, about 2 minutes per side. Drain fritters on paper towels.

Fan avocado slices and grapefruit and orange segments on plates. Drizzle 1 tablespoon sauce over each plate. Top each with 1 fritter. Sprinkle cilantro and chives over and serve.

6 SERVINGS

Crudités with Mediterranean Relish

◆ ◆ ◆

2	teaspoons olive oil
1	cup finely chopped onion
1	tablespoon chopped garlic
1	cup canned crushed tomatoes with added puree
1	teaspoon fresh lemon juice
¼	cup coarsely chopped drained oil-packed sun-dried tomatoes
¼	cup pitted green olives (about 10)
¼	cup (packed) fresh basil leaves
4	large drained canned artichoke hearts
2	tablespoons chopped fresh parsley
2	tablespoons toasted pine nuts
	Assorted vegetables

Heat oil in medium nonstick skillet over medium heat. Add onion and sauté until just beginning to soften, about 3 minutes. Add garlic; sauté 30 seconds. Stir in canned tomatoes and lemon juice. Bring to simmer. Remove from heat.

Combine sun-dried tomatoes and next 5 ingredients in processor. Process until vegetables are finely chopped. Transfer to medium bowl. Stir in tomato mixture. Season with salt and pepper. *(Can be made 1 day ahead. Cover and chill.)* Serve with vegetables.

6 SERVINGS

◆ ◆ ◆

The relish is a good option for those who are watching their calories, fat and cholesterol. Scooping it into a cup made from radicchio leaves is an inventive and attractive serving option. Offer the relish at room temperature for the best flavor.

◆ ◆ ◆

Sweet Chili-glazed Chicken Wings

◆ ◆ ◆

2	pounds chicken wings
¼	cup peanut oil
3	tablespoons finely chopped fresh cilantro
3	tablespoons soy sauce
2½	tablespoons minced garlic
2	tablespoons minced ginger
¾	teaspoon dried crushed red pepper
1	cup rice vinegar
¾	cup sugar
½	cup water
1	tablespoon chili-garlic sauce
	Steamed white rice
¼	cup thinly sliced green onions

Cut each chicken wing in half at joint. Mix peanut oil, cilantro, soy sauce, 2 tablespoons garlic, ginger and ¼ teaspoon crushed red pepper in large bowl. Add chicken wings to oil mixture and turn to coat. Cover and refrigerate 2 hours.

Preheat oven to 400°F. Using tongs, transfer chicken wings to large baking sheet. Bake chicken wings until cooked through and golden brown, about 20 minutes.

Meanwhile, combine vinegar, sugar, water, chili-garlic sauce, remaining ½ tablespoon garlic and remaining ½ teaspoon crushed red pepper in medium saucepan. Bring to boil; reduce heat and simmer until glaze thickens to syrup consistency, about 20 minutes.

Transfer baked chicken wings to large bowl. Pour glaze over; toss to coat. Place chicken wings atop steamed white rice. Sprinkle with green onions and serve.

4 SERVINGS

Rösti with Gruyère Cheese

◆ ◆ ◆

4   bacon slices, chopped
2   cups (packed) shredded peeled russet potatoes (about 2 large)

2   tablespoons (¼ stick) butter
½   cup grated Gruyère cheese (about 2 ounces)

Cook bacon in large nonstick skillet over medium-high heat until crisp, about 8 minutes. Using slotted spoon, transfer bacon to large bowl (reserve drippings in skillet). Add potatoes to bacon; toss to combine. Sprinkle with salt and pepper.

Preheat broiler. Melt butter in same skillet with bacon drippings over medium heat. Form potato mixture into four 4-inch-diameter patties. Add patties to skillet. Cook until golden brown and cooked through, about 6 minutes per side. Transfer patties to baking sheet. Sprinkle cheese atop each. Broil patties until cheese melts, about 1 minute. Transfer to plates and serve.

4 SERVINGS

◆ ◆ ◆

Shredded potatoes, crunchy bacon and melted Gruyère cheese combine perfectly in this popular Swiss dish. It would also be delicious as a light entrée when teamed with a salad.

◆ ◆ ◆

Black-eyed Pea Cakes with Jalapeño Sour Cream

◆ ◆ ◆

1 cup dried black-eyed peas

3 cups water

¾ cup milk (do not use low-fat or nonfat)
½ cup finely chopped onion
3 tablespoons fresh lime juice
½ teaspoon hot pepper sauce (such as Tabasco)
1 cup all purpose flour
¾ teaspoon baking powder
¼ teaspoon baking soda
1 large egg

⅓ cup sour cream
1 tablespoon minced seeded jalapeño chilies

2 teaspoons (about) vegetable oil

Purchased medium-hot red salsa

Place dried black-eyed peas in medium pot. Add enough cold water to cover by 3 inches; let stand overnight. Drain peas.

Return peas to pot. Add 3 cups water. Cover; simmer until peas are tender, stirring occasionally, about 40 minutes. Drain peas, reserving ⅓ cup cooking liquid.

Transfer 1¼ cups peas to processor and puree until smooth, adding enough reserved cooking liquid 1 tablespoon at a time to help blend. Transfer puree to large bowl. Mix in milk, onion, lime juice, hot pepper sauce and remaining whole peas. Stir in flour, baking powder and baking soda. Season with salt and pepper. Mix in egg. Cover and chill batter 30 minutes.

Mix sour cream and jalapeño chilies in small bowl. Let stand 30 minutes at room temperature.

Preheat oven to 250°F. Heat ½ teaspoon oil in heavy large skillet over medium-low heat. Using 1½ tablespoons batter for each pancake, spoon batter into skillet. Cook until bubbles atop pancakes break and batter is almost set, about 3 minutes. Turn pancakes over; cook until cooked through. Transfer pancakes to baking sheet; keep warm in oven. Repeat with remaining batter, adding more oil to skillet as needed, making 24 pancakes.

Spoon salsa onto plates. Arrange 4 pancakes alongside salsa on each plate. Top with sour cream mixture and serve.

6 SERVINGS

Crostini with
Spiced Crab and Shrimp Salad

◆ ◆ ◆

½ cup bottled clam juice
10 ounces medium uncooked shrimp, peeled, deveined

2 cups thinly sliced green onions
⅔ cup mayonnaise
4 teaspoons fresh lemon juice
2 garlic cloves, finely chopped
1 teaspoon Hungarian sweet paprika
½ teaspoon cayenne pepper
8 ounces flaked crabmeat (about 2 cups lightly packed)

⅓ cup (about) olive oil
40 ¼-inch-thick diagonal slices sourdough baguette

Lemon wedges

Bring clam juice to simmer in large skillet over medium heat. Add shrimp; cover and simmer until opaque, turning once, about 2 minutes. Using slotted spoon, transfer shrimp to cutting board; coarsely chop shrimp. Place shrimp in small bowl. Boil cooking liquid until reduced to 2 tablespoons, about 2 minutes. Cool.

Mix onions and next 5 ingredients in large bowl to blend. Stir in shrimp, cooking liquid and crabmeat. Season with salt and pepper. Cover seafood salad and refrigerate.

Preheat oven to 375°F. Lightly brush oil over both sides of each bread slice. Arrange bread on baking sheet in single layer. Bake until bread is crisp and golden, about 4 minutes per side. Cool. *(Seafood salad and toasts can be made 1 day ahead. Keep seafood salad chilled. Store toasts airtight at room temperature.)*

Spread seafood salad evenly over toasts. Arrange on serving dish. Garnish with lemon wedges and serve.

MAKES 40

◆ ◆ ◆

Shrimp and crabmeat pair up in this elegant hors d'oeuvre. The crostini are ideal for entertaining since they can be made up to a day ahead.

◆ ◆ ◆

ABOUT CAVIAR

Caviar is a delicacy that adds a touch of elegance to any occasion. Legally, only sturgeon eggs (roe) may be labeled *caviar*, which is a word derived from the Turkish *havyar* or "egg." Of the many sturgeon species in the world, three kinds—all found in the Caspian Sea—are said to produce the finest caviar.

These three sturgeon are the beluga, the osetra and the sevruga. The beluga produces the largest (pea-size) eggs, which range in color from pale gray to jet black; osetra eggs are medium-sized and gray to gray-green; and sevruga caviar is the smallest and gray. (There actually is a fourth kind of sturgeon called the sterlet, which yields "golden" caviar that has been coveted by shahs and czars throughout history. It's so rare, though, that only billionaires need bother.)

These types of caviar can be quite expensive, but there are other kinds of fish roe on the market, including salmon or red caviar (orange to red, medium-size eggs); lumpfish caviar (very small, black, hard eggs); and whitefish caviar (also called American golden for its small yellow eggs).

◆ ◆ ◆

Artichoke Bottoms with Crème Fraîche and Caviar

◆ ◆ ◆

⅓ cup crème fraîche or sour cream
3 tablespoons chopped green onions (green part only)
2½ tablespoons chopped fresh basil
1 teaspoon grated lemon peel

6 canned artichoke bottoms, drained (patted dry)
1 2-ounce jar salmon caviar
   Fresh basil sprigs

Mix first 4 ingredients in small bowl. Season with salt and pepper. *(Filling can be made 1 day ahead. Cover and refrigerate.)*
Spoon filling onto artichokes. Top each with 1 teaspoon caviar. Garnish artichokes with fresh basil sprigs.

6 SERVINGS

Creamy Oregano Dip with Vegetables

◆ ◆ ◆

3 cups plain nonfat yogurt

2 tablespoons chopped fresh oregano
½ teaspoon dried oregano
1 teaspoon grated lemon peel
1 teaspoon fresh lemon juice
½ teaspoon salt
½ teaspoon pepper
⅛ teaspoon cayenne pepper

2 heads Belgian endive, separated into spears
1 12-ounce basket cherry tomatoes

Set strainer over 4-cup measuring cup. Line strainer with paper towel. Add yogurt to strainer; refrigerate until yogurt is thick (about 1 cup liquid will drain from yogurt into measuring cup), at least 2 hours or overnight.

Turn yogurt out into medium bowl; discard paper towel and drained liquid. Add chopped fresh and dried oregano, lemon peel, lemon juice, salt, pepper and cayenne to yogurt and stir to blend. Cover; chill to develop flavors, at least 2 hours and up to 6 hours.

Place bowl with dip on platter. Surround with endive spears and cherry tomatoes and serve.

6 SERVINGS (ABOUT 1¾ CUPS OF DIP)

Tomato and Mozzarella Bruschetta

◆ ◆ ◆

12 4½ x 2½-inch slices (each ¾ inch thick) crusty French bread
2   garlic cloves, halved
3   tablespoons olive oil
2   teaspoons balsamic vinegar
1   8-ounce ball fresh mozzarella cheese, cut into twelve
    ¼-inch-thick slices
24 ¼-inch-thick slices plum tomatoes
12 fresh basil leaves

Preheat broiler. Broil bread until brown, about 1 minute per side. Rub cut side of garlic over bread. Mix oil and vinegar in small bowl. Brush mixture over bread. Top each bread slice with 1 slice of cheese, 2 tomato slices and 1 basil leaf. Sprinkle with salt and pepper. Arrange on platter and serve.

12 SERVINGS

White Bean, Escarole and Bell Pepper Soup

◆ ◆ ◆

2	tablespoons olive oil
1	large onion, chopped
1	yellow bell pepper, coarsely chopped
1	red bell pepper, coarsely chopped
½	medium head escarole, sliced
⅛	teaspoon dried crushed red pepper
4½	cups canned low-salt chicken broth
1	15-ounce can cannellini (white kidney beans), rinsed, drained
1½	teaspoons dried marjoram
	Grated pecorino Romano cheese

Heat oil in heavy large pot over medium-high heat. Add onion and bell peppers; sauté until beginning to brown, about 15 minutes. Add escarole and crushed red pepper; sauté until escarole wilts, about 3 minutes. Add broth, beans and marjoram. Simmer 10 minutes. Season with salt and pepper. Sprinkle with cheese.

6 SERVINGS

Escarole is part of the endive family. With its broad leaves and mild flavor, this is a green that takes well to salads. Escarole can also be cooked until it wilts and added to soups, such as the hearty bean version here.

◆ ◆ ◆

Yukon Gold Potato and Chive Soup

◆ ◆ ◆

7   cups (or more) canned low-salt chicken broth
2½   pounds Yukon Gold potatoes, peeled, sliced (about 7 cups)
3   large garlic cloves, peeled

⅔   cup half and half
½   cup minced fresh chives

     Sour cream

Combine 7 cups chicken broth, potatoes and garlic cloves in large pot. Bring to boil. Reduce heat to medium; cover and simmer until potatoes are very tender, about 25 minutes.

Working in batches, puree soup in blender until smooth. Return to same pot. Add half and half and bring to simmer. Thin with more broth if soup is too thick. Season to taste with salt and pepper. Stir in chives. *(Can be prepared 1 day ahead. Cover and refrigerate. Rewarm over low heat, stirring frequently.)*

Ladle soup into bowls. Top with dollop of sour cream and serve.

6 SERVINGS

ALL ABOUT CHIVES

Consider the baked potato. Then imagine that baked potato topped with sour cream and chives, its rich and complex flavor belying the simplicity of those three straightforward ingredients. That's what chives do to certain foods: bring out the best in everything from omelets and other egg dishes to soups and salads, creamy sauces and savory butters.

In a few cases, the addition of chives to a particular dish made culinary history. This happened when cooked potatoes and leeks were pureed, chilled and topped with chives for vichyssoise. And again, when a creamy salad dressing was enlivened with tarragon, a few anchovies and a goodly amount of chopped chives, and then christened "green goddess."

Chives have a history of their own, one that dates back nearly five thousand years. They also have a taste that's uniquely theirs, with some describing it as a little like a mild onion and others calling it a cross between onion and garlic. It's a flavor that melds well with other herbs: When mixed with chervil, tarragon and parsley, the fragrant and flavorful result is known as *fines herbes*.

◆ ◆ ◆

Butternut Squash and Corn Chowder

◆ ◆ ◆

2   1-pound butternut squash, peeled, halved lengthwise
7½   cups (or more) water
1   tablespoon salt
½   teaspoon plus 3 tablespoons olive oil

2   cups chopped onions
2   cups frozen corn kernels
2   teaspoons chopped garlic
1   teaspoon ground coriander
¾   teaspoon ground cardamom
½   teaspoon ground cumin
½   teaspoon cayenne pepper
⅛   teaspoon ground cloves

1   large potato, peeled, cut into ½-inch pieces

Preheat oven to 400°F. Using spoon, scrape out seeds from squash; reserve seeds. Combine 1½ cups water, squash seeds and 1 tablespoon salt in small saucepan. Bring to boil. Strain seeds; rinse under cold water to remove any squash pieces from seeds. Pat seeds dry with paper towel. Toss seeds with ½ teaspoon oil in small bowl. Sprinkle with salt. Transfer to baking sheet. Place squash on baking sheet. Brush with 1 tablespoon oil. Roast seeds until toasted, about 6 minutes. Roast squash until tender and lightly browned, turning once, about 45 minutes. Cut into ¾-inch pieces.

Heat 2 tablespoons oil in heavy large pot over medium-high heat. Add chopped onions, 1⅓ cups corn, garlic, coriander, cardamom, cumin, cayenne and cloves; sauté until onions are tender, about 8 minutes. Add squash and 6 cups water. Bring to boil. Reduce heat and simmer chowder for 30 minutes.

Working in batches, puree chowder in processor until smooth. Return chowder to same pot. Bring to boil. Reduce heat. Add potato and remaining ⅔ cup corn kernels; simmer until potato is cooked through, thinning chowder with more water if necessary, about 12 minutes. Season with salt and pepper. Spoon chowder into bowls. Garnish with toasted squash seeds and serve.

6 SERVINGS

◆ ◆ ◆

A spice combination that is inspired by Indian cuisine enhances this sensational recipe. The seeds of the butternut squash are toasted and used to garnish the chunky soup.

◆ ◆ ◆

Quick Shrimp Bisque

◆ ◆ ◆

2 tablespoons (¼ stick) butter
¾ cup chopped onion
1¾ cups bottled clam juice
3 tablespoons long-grain white rice
12 ounces cooked peeled deveined medium shrimp

3 tablespoons tomato paste
⅛ teaspoon (or more) cayenne pepper
1¼ cups half and half

Melt butter in heavy medium saucepan over medium heat. Add onion and sauté until tender, about 4 minutes. Add clam juice and rice and bring to boil. Reduce heat to low, cover and simmer until rice is tender, about 15 minutes. Mix in shrimp. Cover and simmer soup until shrimp are heated through, about 1 minute longer. Set aside 6 shrimp for garnish.

Working in batches, puree soup with remaining shrimp in blender until smooth. Return soup to same saucepan. Whisk in tomato paste and ⅛ teaspoon cayenne pepper. Gradually whisk in half and half. Bring soup to simmer. Season with salt and pepper.

Ladle soup into bowls. Garnish with reserved shrimp. Sprinkle with additional cayenne pepper, if desired, and serve.

2 SERVINGS

◆ ◆ ◆

A bisque is a rich, thick soup made with pureed seafood (and sometimes poultry or vegetables) and cream. In this easy recipe, half and half replaces heavy cream without sacraficing either the soup's texture or the taste.

◆ ◆ ◆

Yam Soup with Coriander

◆ ◆ ◆

¼   cup plain nonfat yogurt
2   tablespoons (packed) chopped fresh cilantro
½   small garlic clove, minced

     Nonstick vegetable oil spray
1½   pounds yams (red-skinned sweet potatoes), peeled,
     cut into 1-inch-thick slices

3¾   cups (or more) low-fat (1%) milk
1½   teaspoons ground coriander

Mix yogurt, cilantro and garlic in small bowl. Cover; chill.

Preheat oven to 400°F. Spray large baking sheet (preferably nonstick) with vegetable oil spray. Arrange yam slices in single layer on prepared baking sheet. Roast until bottom sides of yam slices are brown, about 20 minutes. Turn yam slices over and roast until tender, about 15 minutes longer.

Meanwhile, combine 2 cups milk and coriander in heavy medium saucepan. Bring to simmer. Reduce heat to very low; cover and cook 10 minutes. Remove from heat.

Combine yams and milk mixture in processor. Puree until smooth. Return to same saucepan. Stir in remaining 1¾ cups milk and bring to simmer, thinning with more milk, if desired. Season to taste with salt and pepper. *(Yogurt mixture and soup can be prepared 1 day ahead. Cover separately and refrigerate. Rewarm soup over medium heat before continuing.)*

Ladle soup into bowls. Swirl 1 tablespoonful of yogurt mixture into each bowl and serve immediately.

4 SERVINGS

◆ ◆ ◆

Complex carbohydrates found in grains and some vegetables supply the calories needed for energy and the vitamins, minerals and fiber needed for overall good health. This low-fat soup made from roasted yams is a delicious way to add more complex carbohydrates to your diet.

◆ ◆ ◆

Thai Red Curry Soup with Chicken and Vegetables

♦ ♦ ♦

2 tablespoons corn oil
1 tablespoon Thai red curry paste*
12 ounces skinless boneless chicken breast halves, cut crosswise into ½-inch-wide strips
4 ounces green beans, cut into 1-inch pieces
2 small Japanese eggplants, cut into 1-inch pieces
3 cups canned low-salt chicken broth
3 cups canned unsweetened coconut milk*
1 tablespoon fish sauce (nam pla)*
¼ cup chopped fresh basil

Heat oil in heavy large saucepan over medium heat. Add curry paste; stir until fragrant, about 1 minute. Add chicken; stir 2 minutes. Add green bean and eggplant pieces; stir 1 minute. Add broth, coconut milk and fish sauce; bring to boil. Reduce heat and simmer until vegetables are tender, about 12 minutes. Season with salt and pepper. Stir in basil and serve.

These ingredients are available at Asian markets and in the Asian foods section of some supermarkets.

4 SERVINGS

♦ ♦ ♦

Chili paste is an ingredient that has become increasingly popular in recent times. Here, it is used to spice up a silken, coconut-flavored soup.

♦ ♦ ♦

Country-Style Bean and Vegetable Soup

◆ ◆ ◆

Creativity with simple ingredients is a hallmark of Sicilian cooking, with this bean and vegetable soup illustrating the concept perfectly. Some say that the soup evolved from a dish that fifteenth-century galley cooks once made for mariners.

◆ ◆ ◆

½ cup dried fava beans*
½ cup dried Great Northern beans

6 cups water
1 large onion, finely chopped
1 carrot, peeled, finely chopped
1 small celery stalk, finely chopped
8 ounces savoy cabbage, cut into 1-inch pieces (about 4 cups)
½ head Bibb lettuce, cut into 1-inch pieces (about 2 cups)
  Freshly grated Parmesan cheese
  Extra-virgin olive oil

Place fava beans in medium saucepan. Place Great Northern beans in large bowl. Add enough cold water to each to cover by 3 inches and let soak overnight.

Bring fava beans to boil in their soaking liquid. Boil 5 minutes. Drain fava beans and cool slightly. Using small sharp knife, make small slit in skin of each fava bean. Peel off outer skins and discard. Drain Great Northern beans.

Bring 6 cups water to boil in large pot. Add all beans, onion, carrot and celery. Partially cover; simmer over medium heat until beans are half cooked, about 30 minutes. Add cabbage and lettuce. Partially cover; cook until beans are tender, stirring occasionally, about 1 hour. Season with salt and pepper. Ladle into bowls. Sprinkle with Parmesan. Drizzle with oil and serve.

Available at Italian markets, Middle Eastern markets, specialty foods stores and some supermarkets.

4 SERVINGS

Roasted Tomato and Red Bell Pepper Soup

◆ ◆ ◆

2¼ pounds tomatoes, halved lengthwise
2 large red bell peppers, quartered, seeded
1 onion, cut into thin wedges

◆ ◆ ◆

A rich and satisfying soup with great roasted tomato flavor. Served cold here, it would also be good hot or even at room temperature.

◆ ◆ ◆

4   large garlic cloves, peeled
2   tablespoons olive oil (preferably extra-virgin)

1   teaspoon fresh thyme leaves or ½ teaspoon dried
2   cups (about) water

4   tablespoons part-skim ricotta cheese, room temperature
        Fresh thyme sprigs (optional)

Preheat oven to 450°F. Arrange tomatoes (cut side up), bell peppers, onion and garlic cloves on large baking sheet. Drizzle oil over; sprinkle generously with salt and pepper. Roast vegetables until brown and tender, turning peppers and onion occasionally, approximately 40 minutes. Remove from oven. Cool.

Transfer vegetables and any accumulated juices to processor. Add thyme leaves. Puree soup, gradually adding enough water to thin soup to desired consistency. Chill until cold, about 3 hours. *(Can be prepared 1 day ahead. Cover and keep refrigerated. If soup becomes too thick, thin with water to desired consistency.)*

Ladle soup into bowls. Top each with 1 tablespoon ricotta cheese. Garnish with thyme sprigs, if desired, and serve.

4 SERVINGS

Fennel, Leek and Spinach Soup

◆ ◆ ◆

6   tablespoons (¾ stick) margarine
6   cups chopped fresh fennel bulbs
4   cups chopped leeks (white and pale green parts only)
6   cups canned low-salt chicken broth

⅔   cup (packed) fresh spinach leaves

Melt margarine in large pot over medium heat. Add fennel and leeks. Sauté until just translucent, about 15 minutes. Add broth and cover pot. Simmer until vegetables are tender, about 20 minutes.

Puree soup in small batches in blender until smooth, adding spinach to last batch before pureeing. Return soup to same pot. Season with salt and pepper. *(Can be prepared 1 day ahead. Refrigerate until cold, then cover and keep refrigerated.)*

Rewarm soup over low heat, stirring occasionally. Ladle into bowls and serve soup immediately.

8 SERVINGS

Creamy Carrot Soup

◆ ◆ ◆

5   large carrots (about 1½ pounds), peeled, cut into ½-inch pieces
3½   cups canned low-salt chicken broth
1   large onion, peeled, quartered
1¼   teaspoons chopped fresh thyme or ½ teaspoon dried
1   large bay leaf
¼   teaspoon (scant) ground allspice

¾   cup drained canned small white beans
1   cup milk

Combine carrots, broth, onion, thyme, bay leaf and allspice in large pot and bring to boil. Reduce heat, cover and simmer until carrots are tender, about 15 minutes. Remove bay leaf.

This pretty soup, served in larger portions, could be a soothing lunch or a light dinner—and it's healthful, too.

◆ ◆ ◆

Working in batches, puree soup in blender until smooth, adding some of beans with each batch. Return soup to same pot; add milk. Stir over low heat until heated through. Season to taste with salt and pepper. Ladle soup into bowls and serve.

6 TO 8 SERVINGS

Mexican Lime Soup

◆ ◆ ◆

2	tablespoons olive oil
6	garlic cloves, sliced
6	small skinless boneless chicken breast halves, cut crosswise into 1/2-inch-wide strips
1 1/2	teaspoons dried oregano
9	cups canned low-salt chicken broth
1/3	cup fresh lime juice
1 1/2	cups coarsely crushed tortilla chips
2	avocados, pitted, peeled, diced
3	tomatoes, chopped
3	green onions, sliced
	Chopped fresh cilantro
	Minced jalapeño chilies
	Lime slices

Heat oil in heavy large pot over medium heat. Add garlic and stir until fragrant, about 20 seconds. Add chicken and oregano to pot; sprinkle with salt and pepper. Sauté 3 minutes. Add broth and lime juice and bring to simmer. Reduce heat to medium-low and simmer gently until chicken is cooked through, about 8 minutes. Season soup to taste with salt and pepper.

Divide crushed tortilla chips among 6 bowls. Ladle soup into bowls. Top soup with avocados, tomatoes, green onions, cilantro and jalapeños. Garnish with lime slices and serve.

6 SERVINGS

A homey yet sophisticated soup that's great for casual entertaining. Strips of chicken give it substance, while chopped avocado, tomatoes, green onions, cilantro and jalapeños make interesting toppings.

◆ ◆ ◆

Here's a refreshing cumin-laced zucchini soup that's perfect for hot-weather meals. It definitely won't weigh you down, with only 3 grams of fat and 89 calories per serving.

◆ ◆ ◆

Chilled Zucchini-Cumin Soup

◆ ◆ ◆

1	teaspoon olive oil
1	large onion, chopped
1½	teaspoons ground cumin
1½	pounds zucchini, trimmed, cut into ¾-inch pieces
2	14½-ounce cans low-salt chicken broth
⅓	cup chopped fresh basil
4	tablespoons plain nonfat yogurt
	Sliced fresh basil

Heat oil in heavy medium saucepan over medium heat. Add onion and sauté until tender about 5 minutes. Add cumin and stir until aromatic, about 30 seconds. Mix in zucchini. Add broth; bring soup to boil. Reduce heat and simmer until zucchini is very tender, about 30 minutes. Cool soup slightly.

Mix ⅓ cup chopped basil into soup. Working in batches, puree soup in blender until smooth. Transfer to bowl. Season with salt and pepper. Cover and refrigerate until cold, about 3 hours. *(Can be made 1 day ahead. Keep refrigerated.)*

Ladle soup into bowls. Top each with 1 tablespoon plain nonfat yogurt and sliced fresh basil and serve.

4 SERVINGS

Pineapple and Bell Pepper Gazpacho

◆ ◆ ◆

2	cups chopped cored peeled pineapple
2	cups chopped seeded peeled cucumber
1½	cups pineapple juice
⅔	cup chopped red bell pepper
⅔	cup chopped yellow bell pepper
6	tablespoons chopped Maui onion or other sweet onion
3	tablespoons chopped Italian parsley
4	teaspoons minced jalapeño chili

Additional diced bell pepper and seeded cucumber (for garnish)

Puree first 8 ingredients in blender until smooth. Transfer to bowl. Cover and refrigerate until cold, at least 2 hours or up to 6 hours. Season to taste with salt and pepper.

Ladle soup into bowls. Sprinkle with additional chopped bell pepper and cucumber and serve.

4 SERVINGS

◆ ◆ ◆

Gazpacho is a cold soup that originated in southern Spain. Traditionally, it is made from a puree of fresh tomatoes, bell peppers, onions, celery and cucumber. In this version, pineapple replaces the tomatoes.

◆ ◆ ◆

Bourbon-Grapefruit Highball

◆ ◆ ◆

    Ice cubes
6   tablespoons bourbon
10   dashes Angostura bitters
1½ cups grapefruit soda

Fill two 14- to 16-ounce glasses with ice. Divide bourbon and bitters, then soda between glasses. Stir to blend.

2 SERVINGS

Raspberry Vodka

◆ ◆ ◆

3   10-ounce packages frozen raspberries in syrup, thawed
3   tablespoons sugar
2   cups vodka

1   orange

Place raspberries in strainer set over large bowl. Let stand 10 minutes (do not mash berries). Transfer juice to medium saucepan. Add sugar to juice and stir over low heat until sugar dissolves. Remove from heat. Stir in vodka. Pour vodka mixture into 5-cup jar or bottle. Add strained berries.

Using small sharp knife, cut peel from orange. Cut white pith from peel and discard. Cut peel into ¼-inch-wide strips. Add peel to vodka. Place lid on container; seal tightly. Refrigerate vodka at least 4 days and up to 3 months.

MAKES ABOUT 4 CUPS

◆ ◆ ◆

Moscow's favorite drink is sweetened with raspberries and sugar in this easy-to-make recipe. It's terrific drizzled over vanilla ice cream or served as a cocktail on its own.

◆ ◆ ◆

Frozen Mango Martini

◆ ◆ ◆

½   cup sugar

½   cup water

1   1¼-inch-long piece fresh ginger (about 1 inch in diameter), sliced

2   medium mangoes, peeled, pitted

½   cup vodka

20 ice cubes

Combine sugar, water and ginger in heavy small saucepan. Stir over medium heat until sugar dissolves. Simmer 5 minutes. Remove from heat. Cover; let steep 1 hour. Strain ginger syrup. Cool. *(Can be made 1 day ahead. Cover and refrigerate.)*

Puree mangoes in blender. Pour into measuring cup. Return ¾ cup puree to blender (reserve any remaining puree for another use). Add ½ cup ginger syrup (reserve any remaining syrup for another use), vodka and ice cubes to blender. Blend until smooth.

MAKES 4

MARTINI MADNESS

The classic Martini has had competition of late, as alternative takes on the traditional gin and vermouth cocktail have spread like wildfire through clubs, lounges and bars across the land. There is the Sapphire Martini, made with Bombay Sapphire and blue curaçao; the orange Martini, a combination of Stolichnaya Ohranj, bitters, triple sec and orange juice; and the Dirty Martini with olive juice clouding the usually clear drink.

Amidst the clutter, it is easy to forget what a proper Martini is: gin, vermouth and either an olive or a twist of lemon peel. After that, though, the "proper" of Martini making gets increasingly murky. Most Martini experts (i.e. anyone who drinks them religiously) contend that the glass, the shaker and the gin must be chilled. The proportion of gin to vermouth varies from a whisper of vermouth (passing the cork over the shaker counts) to nearly a third vermouth to gin. Regardless of proportion, the gin and vermouth are shaken over ice and then strained into a chilled, triangle-shaped glass, with olives or lemon peel added to taste. Whatever the trend of the moment, the classic Martini will always be cool.

◆ ◆ ◆

Champagne Framboise

◆ ◆ ◆

Ice cubes
12 tablespoons framboise (raspberry liqueur)
8   teaspoons fresh lemon juice
1½ 750-ml bottles (about) chilled brut Champagne
¾   cup fresh raspberries (about 24)

Fill 8 Champagne flutes with ice cubes. Pour 1½ tablespoons framboise into each flute. Add 1 teaspoon lemon juice to each. Fill flutes with Champagne. Garnish with raspberries and serve.

8 SERVINGS

◆ ◆ ◆

Champagne is, of course, the classic celebratory drink, but the bubbly is made even more festive here with the addition of framboise (raspberry liqueur) and fresh raspberries.

◆ ◆ ◆

Hot Spiced Apple-Raspberry Cider

◆ ◆ ◆

8   quarter-size pieces crystallized ginger
4   cinnamon sticks
12 whole cloves
12 whole allspice
8   cups apple cider
2   12-ounce cans frozen apple-grape-raspberry juice concentrate
3   cups water
2   cups orange juice

Wrap ginger, cinnamon sticks, cloves and allspice in cheesecloth; tie to secure. Place in large pot. Add apple cider and all remaining ingredients and bring to boil. Reduce heat and simmer 45 minutes to blend flavors. Remove spices. Ladle cider into mugs and serve.

12 SERVINGS

Hot Chocolate with Espresso, Lemon and Anise

◆ ◆ ◆

4   cups milk (do not use low-fat or nonfat)
¾   cup sugar
4   ounces unsweetened chocolate, finely chopped

2   ounces semisweet chocolate, finely chopped
2   tablespoons instant espresso powder
5   ½-inch-wide strips lemon peel
6   tablespoons anise-flavored liqueur (such as sambuca)

Combine all ingredients except liqueur in large saucepan. Whisk over medium-high heat until chocolate melts and mixture is smooth and comes to boil. Remove from heat; mix in liqueur. Divide among cups and serve.

4 TO 6 SERVINGS

Mocha-Cinnamon Café au Lait

◆ ◆ ◆

2   cups low-fat (2%) milk
3   cinnamon sticks
20   whole cloves
5   ounces imported milk chocolate, chopped
2   ounces bittersweet (not unsweetened) or semisweet chocolate, chopped

3   cups freshly brewed strong coffee
3   tablespoons golden brown sugar
1½   teaspoons vanilla extract

½   cup chilled whipping cream
     Ground nutmeg

Combine milk, cinnamon sticks and whole cloves in medium saucepan. Bring to simmer. Remove from heat. Add both chocolates and whisk until melted. Cover and let stand 15 minutes.

Bring milk mixture to simmer. Add coffee, 2 tablespoons sugar and 1 teaspoon vanilla; stir over medium-low heat until flavors blend (do not boil), about 5 minutes.

Meanwhile, beat cream, pinch of nutmeg, 1 tablespoon sugar and ½ teaspoon vanilla in small bowl until soft peaks form.

Strain coffee; ladle into mugs. Top with whipped cream. Sprinkle with more nutmeg and serve.

6 SERVINGS

THE BUZZ ON COFFEE

Coffee is hot—and we're not just talking temperature. These days there's a coffeehouse on every block, each one serving a seemingly endless variety of coffee drinks. How to choose? Here's a guide to some of the most popular ones around.

◆ *Café au lait:* A French term for "coffee with milk," it's made with equal parts coffee and heated milk.

◆ *Espresso:* Steam is forced through finely ground, dark-roasted coffee beans; the result is a coffee so strong that it is usually served in small (demitasse) cups.

◆ *Caffè latte:* Similar to café au lait, a caffè latte starts with a shot of espresso (usually about one-third of the coffee cup), followed by steamed milk to fill the cup. It's topped with a layer of foamy milk.

◆ *Cappuccino:* The cup is filled with one part espresso, followed by equal parts steamed milk and foam.

◆ *Caffè mocha:* Chocolate syrup is partnered with espresso and steamed milk; it's often topped with whipped cream and sweetened chocolate powder.

◆ *Caffè macchiato:* Macchiato means "stained" in Italian, which is how this espresso drink looks when foam from steamed milk is added.

◆ ◆ ◆

White Chocolate Cappuccino

◆ ◆ ◆

4 cups milk (do not use low-fat or nonfat)
1 vanilla bean, split lengthwise
10 ounces good-quality white chocolate (such as Lindt or Baker's), chopped
2½ teaspoons brandy
2½ teaspoons vanilla extract

4 cups hot, very strong fresh-brewed coffee
Unsweetened cocoa powder

Place milk in heavy medium saucepan. Scrape in seeds from vanilla bean; add bean. Bring to boil. Remove from heat. Add white chocolate and whisk until melted and smooth. Whisk in brandy and vanilla extract. Using tongs, remove bean. Return mixture to low heat and whisk until frothy, 1 minute.

Pour hot coffee into mugs. Ladle white chocolate mixture over. Sprinkle with cocoa powder and serve.

8 SERVINGS

Iced Tea Sangria with Fresh Fruit

◆ ◆ ◆

4   cups water
2   tea bags
4   to 5 tablespoons sugar

1   peach or apple, peeled, pitted or seeded, chopped
4   large strawberries, hulled, halved
1   orange, all peel and white pith removed, cut into ¾-inch pieces
1   cup dry red wine
     Ice cubes

Bring water to boil in medium saucepan. Remove from heat. Add tea bags; steep 3 minutes. Remove tea bags; pour tea into pitcher. Add sugar to taste and stir until sugar dissolves. Cool. *(Can be made 1 day ahead. Cover and refrigerate.)*

Mix fruit in bowl. Divide among four 16-ounce glasses. Pour ¼ cup wine, then 1 cup tea into each glass. Fill glasses with ice cubes.

4 SERVINGS

◆ ◆ ◆

This is a refreshing drink for the cocktail hour. Use any kind of black tea you like; fruit-flavored ones are particularly nice in this recipe.

◆ ◆ ◆

Spirited Hot Apple Cider

◆ ◆ ◆

1   orange
3   tablespoons unsalted butter
¼   cup firmly packed brown sugar
3   cinnamon sticks
10   whole allspice
10   whole cloves
6   cups apple cider
¼   cup dark rum
½   cup applejack
     Additional cinnamon sticks (optional)

Using vegetable peeler, remove peel (orange part only) in strips from orange. Melt butter in heavy large saucepan over medium heat. Add peel, sugar, 3 cinnamon sticks, allspice and cloves; stir 1 minute. Add cider; bring to simmer. Reduce heat to low; simmer 15 minutes. Mix in rum and applejack. Strain into mugs. Garnish with additional cinnamon sticks, if desired.

6 TO 8 SERVINGS

·MAIN COURSES·

*Clockwise from bottom left:
Tomato Salad (page 153);
Potato and Parmesan Gratin
(page 147); and Grilled Veal
Chops with Rosemary (page 57).*

Beef Tenderloin with Salsa Verde

◆ ◆ ◆

3 tablespoons chopped fresh thyme
2 tablespoons coarse salt
1 tablespoon ground pepper
1 2½-pound whole beef tenderloin, trimmed

¾ cup extra-virgin olive oil
2 tablespoons drained capers
2 tablespoons chopped Italian parsley
2 tablespoons chopped shallot

1 tablespoon vegetable oil

Sprinkle 2 tablespoons thyme, coarse salt and pepper on baking sheet. Roll tenderloin in spice mixture. Cover; chill 3 hours.

Mix olive oil, capers, parsley, shallot and 1 tablespoon thyme in bowl. Season with salt and pepper. Let salsa stand 1 hour.

Preheat oven to 400°F. Heat vegetable oil in heavy large skillet over high heat. Add tenderloin; cook until brown on all sides, about 10 minutes. Transfer to baking sheet. Roast until meat thermometer inserted into center of tenderloin registers 125°F for rare, about 12 minutes. Remove tenderloin from oven and let stand 5 minutes. Serve tenderloin with salsa.

6 SERVINGS

A member of the mustard family, horseradish is known for its strong bite and underlying sweetness. Centuries ago, the root was used throughout Europe to prevent scurvy, relieve coughs and treat gout. These days, horseradish appears not in medicine cabinets but on kitchen tables as a zesty flavoring for a number of dishes from around the world.

That potent flavor is best achieved, according to horseradish purists, by grating your own fresh horseradish root, which is available in fall and spring. Many recipes, though, call for convenient (and less pungent) prepared horseradish, which comes in jars.

Bottled horseradish is available in two common varieties: white and red. The white is ground horseradish root that has been preserved in salt and vinegar; the red has added beet juice.

Horseradish often plays a supporting role as a flavoring in sauces of many kinds; but it stars in two special holiday dishes. During Passover, horseradish is used at the traditional seder to represent the bitter herb, called *maror* in Hebrew. At Christmas, creamed horseradish is a traditional accompaniment to that Yuletide classic, roast prime rib of beef.

◆ ◆ ◆

Prime Rib with Roasted Garlic and Horseradish Crust

◆ ◆ ◆

30	large garlic cloves, unpeeled
¼	cup olive oil
⅓	cup prepared white cream-style horseradish
½	teaspoon coarse salt
1	6-pound well-trimmed boneless beef rib roast
	Beet, Red Onion and Horseradish Relish (see recipe below)

Preheat oven to 350°F. Toss garlic cloves and olive oil in small baking dish and cover. Bake until garlic begins to brown, about 35 minutes. Drain olive oil into processor. Cool 15 minutes. Peel garlic and place in processor. Add prepared horseradish and coarse salt. Puree garlic mixture until almost smooth.

Place rack on large rimmed baking sheet. Sprinkle beef with salt and pepper. Spread thin layer of garlic mixture on underside of beef. Place beef, garlic mixture side down, onto rack. Spread top of beef with remaining garlic mixture. Cover beef with plasic wrap and refrigerate at least 3 hours or up to 1 day.

Position rack in bottom third of oven; preheat to 350°F. Uncover beef. Roast until thermometer inserted into top center registers 125°F for rare, about 1 hour 45 minutes. Transfer beef to platter; let stand 30 minutes. Scrape pan juices into small saucepan.

Slice beef crosswise. Rewarm juices; drizzle over beef. Serve with Beet, Red Onion and Horseradish Relish.

8 SERVINGS

Beet, Red Onion and Horseradish Relish

3	2½-inch-diameter beets, trimmed
½	cup olive oil
3	tablespoons balsamic vinegar
1	teaspoon coarse salt
½	teaspoon pepper
1½	cups chopped red onion
⅓	cup prepared white cream-style horseradish

Preheat oven to 350°F. Wrap beets in double thickness of foil. Roast beets on oven rack until tender, about 1 hour 45 minutes. Unwrap beets and let cool completely.

Whisk oil, vinegar, salt and pepper in medium bowl until blended. Mix in onion and horseradish.

Peel beets; cut into ⅓-inch dice. Add to onion mixture. Cover and refrigerate at least 1 day and up to 4 days.

MAKES 4 CUPS

Cowboy Burgers

◆ ◆ ◆

¼	cup mashed drained canned kidney beans
1	pound ground beef (7% fat)
6	tablespoons hickory barbecue sauce
4	teaspoons prepared white horseradish
4	teaspoons minced garlic
½	teaspoon salt
½	teaspoon pepper
4	oversize wheat rolls, halved
4	⅓-inch-thick slices red onion
	Nonstick vegetable oil spray
	Watercress sprigs

Place mashed beans in medium bowl. Mix in next 6 ingredients. Shape into four ½-inch-thick patties.

Prepare barbecue (medium heat). Spray cut sides of rolls and both sides of burgers and onion slices with nonstick spray. Grill cut sides of rolls until toasted, about 1 minute. Transfer rolls to plates. Grill burgers about 4 minutes per side for medium; grill onion slices about 5 minutes per side. Place 1 burger, 1 onion slice and some watercress on each roll bottom. Cover each with roll top.

4 SERVINGS

Here's a hamburger that's low on fat, but high on flavor, thanks to extra-lean ground beef and mashed kidney beans. Plus, these burgers are big enough to satisfy the hungriest of cowboys (and family members, too).

◆ ◆ ◆

Grilled Skirt Steak with Cilantro Chimichurri Sauce

◆ ◆ ◆

The diverse flavors of Central America, Cuba, Brazil and beyond are mixed and matched with those of North American cooking to form a bold new "fusion" cuisine known as "Nuevo Latino." This recipe is an excellent *and* delicious example of the trend. The grilled steak is topped with a *chimichurri* sauce, an herb and vinegar blend typical of Argentine cooking. Serve it with black beans and rice, if you like.

◆ ◆ ◆

½   cup (packed) fresh cilantro leaves
6   garlic cloves
2   jalapeño chilies, stemmed, halved
4   large bay leaves, center stem removed, leaves crumbled
1   tablespoon dried oregano
1   teaspoon salt
1   cup (packed) Italian parsley leaves
½   cup distilled white vinegar
½   cup olive oil

6   5- to 6-ounce skirt steaks
    Tomato wedges (optional)
    Watercress sprigs (optional)

Combine ¼ cup cilantro and next 5 ingredients in processor. Blend until mixture is finely chopped, scraping down bowl occasionally. Add parsley, vinegar, oil and ¼ cup cilantro. Blend until herbs are coarsely chopped. Season with pepper.

Prepare barbecue (medium-high heat) or preheat broiler. Sprinkle steaks with salt and pepper. Cook 3 minutes per side for medium-rare. Transfer to plates. Spoon some sauce over. Garnish with tomatoes and watercress. Pass remaining sauce separately.

6 SERVINGS

Grilled Rib-Eye Steaks with Mediterranean Rub

◆ ◆ ◆

2 tablespoons ground cumin
1 tablespoon ground paprika
1½ teaspoons ground ginger
1½ teaspoons ground coriander
1 teaspoon ground black pepper
¼ teaspoon cayenne pepper
2 tablespoons olive oil
4 1-pound boneless rib-eye steaks (each about
  1¼ inches thick), trimmed

8 lemon wedges

Blend first 6 ingredients in small bowl. Mix in oil to form smooth paste. Rub mixture over steaks. Transfer to baking pan. Cover; chill at least 3 hours or overnight.

Prepare barbecue (medium-high heat). Sprinkle steaks with salt. Grill steaks to desired doneness, about 5 minutes per side for medium-rare. Place on cutting board; let stand 4 minutes. Cut steaks into ½-inch-thick diagonal slices. Transfer to platter. Sprinkle steaks with salt. Serve with lemon wedges.

8 SERVINGS

◆ ◆ ◆

WARM-WEATHER BARBECUE FOR EIGHT

GRILLED RIB-EYE STEAKS WITH
MEDITERRANEAN RUB
(AT LEFT; PICTURED AT LEFT)

GRILLED NEW POTAOTES WITH
PARMESAN AND HERBS
(PAGE 146; PICTURED AT LEFT)

GREEN BEAN AND RADISH SALAD

ASSORTED BEERS

CHERRY UPSIDE-DOWN CAKE
(PAGE 190; PICTURED AT LEFT)

◆ ◆ ◆

Braised Short Ribs with Vegetables

◆ ◆ ◆

1   cup dry white wine
3   tablespoons minced garlic
2   tablespoons Dijon mustard
1   teaspoon dried crushed red pepper
18 3- to 4-inch pieces meaty beef chuck short ribs

3¾ cups beef stock or canned broth

2   tablespoons olive oil
1½ cups finely chopped carrots
1½ cups finely chopped celery
1½ cups finely chopped onions
5¼ cups chicken stock or canned low-salt broth
4   teaspoons chopped fresh thyme
2   bay leaves

4   teaspoons cornstarch
¼   cup water
    Fresh thyme sprigs

Mix wine, 1 tablespoon garlic, mustard and pepper in large glass baking dish. Add short ribs; turn to coat. Cover; chill overnight.

Preheat oven to 500°F. Using tongs, transfer short ribs to large roasting pan; reserve marinade. Sprinkle ribs with salt and pepper. Roast until brown, turning once, about 30 minutes. Transfer short ribs to large bowl. Place pan over 2 burners. Heat over medium-high heat. Add 1 cup beef stock to pan; bring to boil, scraping up any browned bits. Pour juices into bowl with short ribs.

Reduce oven temperature to 350°F. Heat oil in heavy large ovenproof pot over medium-high heat. Add carrots, celery, onions and 2 tablespoons garlic. Sauté until vegetables are tender, about 12 minutes. Add short ribs and pan juices, reserved marinade, 2¾ cups beef stock, chicken stock, thyme and bay leaves. Bring to boil. Cover pot and place in oven. Bake until ribs are tender, about 2 hours.

Using tongs, transfer short ribs to large bowl. Boil cooking liquid until reduced to thin sauce consistency, about 25 minutes. Strain liquid; discard solids and return liquid to pot. Dissolve cornstarch in ¼ cup water. Whisk into cooking liquid. Boil until sauce thickens and coats spoon, stirring constantly, about 2 minutes. Season with pepper. Return ribs to pot. Simmer until heated through, 3 minutes. Transfer to platter. Garnish with thyme.

6 SERVINGS

◆ ◆ ◆

DINNER IN THE KITCHEN FOR SIX

SMOKED SALMON WITH
HORSERADISH CREAM ON
TOAST POINTS

SPARKLING BRUT ROSÉ

BRAISED SHORT RIBS WITH
VEGETABLES
(AT LEFT; PICTURED OPPOSITE)

CRISPY GARLIC RISOTTO CAKES
(PAGE 148; PICTURED OPPOSITE)

RED BELL PEPPER AND
ZUCCHINI SAUTÉ

ZINFANDEL

CHOCOLATE-ORANGE TART
WITH ALMOND CRUST
(PAGE 173)

Skirt Steak Salad with Mushrooms and Chipotle Aioli

◆ ◆ ◆

AIOLI

1	cup mayonnaise
¼	cup coarse-grained Dijon mustard
2	tablespoons white wine vinegar
1	tablespoon minced canned chipotle chilies*

STEAK

½	cup dark beer
¼	cup olive oil
2	tablespoons chopped garlic
2	tablespoons red wine vinegar
1	teaspoon Worcestershire sauce
¾	teaspoon hot pepper sauce (such as Tabasco)
2	pounds skirt steak, trimmed of fat

SALAD

2	red onions, thinly sliced into rounds
2	tablespoons fresh lemon juice
¾	teaspoon coarse salt
3	tablespoons butter
1	large shallot, sliced
¾	pound assorted mushrooms (such as crimini and oyster), sliced
¼	cup Sherry wine vinegar
¼	cup olive oil
10	ounces mixed baby lettuces

FOR AIOLI: Whisk all ingredients in small bowl to blend. Season dressing to taste with salt and pepper. *(Aioli can be prepared 1 day ahead. Cover and refrigerate.)*

FOR STEAK: Whisk first 6 ingredients to blend in 13 x 9 x 2-inch glass baking dish. Add skirt steak to marinade; turn to coat. Cover and refrigerate at least 8 hours.

FOR SALAD: Combine onions, lemon juice and coarse salt in medium bowl. Let stand 1 hour, tossing occasionally.

Prepare barbecue (medium-high heat). Remove steak from marinade. Sprinkle with salt and pepper. Grill about 3 minutes per side for medium-rare. Transfer steak to work surface.

Melt butter in heavy large skillet over medium-high heat.

Add shallot and mushrooms; sauté until well browned, about 7 minutes. Add vinegar to skillet and bring to boil, scraping up browned bits. Remove from heat; mix in oil. Season mushroom mixture to taste with salt and pepper.

Combine lettuces, onions and mushrooms in large bowl; toss. Divide lettuce mixture among 6 plates. Thinly slice steak across grain; arrange atop lettuce mixture. Drizzle some of aioli over salads. Pass remaining aioli separately.

Chipotle chilies in a spicy tomato sauce are sold at Latin markets, specialty foods stores and some supermarkets.

6 SERVINGS

Peppered Beef Slices with Green Onions and Radishes

◆ ◆ ◆

1½   pounds lean flank steak, cut across grain into ¼-inch-wide strips

⅓   cup dry red wine

1   tablespoon sugar

1½   teaspoons coarsely cracked black pepper

1   teaspoon crushed fennel seeds

¾   cup canned low-salt chicken broth

2   tablespoons low-sodium soy sauce

1½   tablespoons cornstarch

3   teaspoons vegetable oil

24   green onions, cut diagonally into 2-inch pieces

24   radishes, cut into ¼-inch-thick slices

Combine first 5 ingredients in 13 x 9 x 2-inch glass baking dish. Cover and refrigerate at least 2 hours, turning once to coat. *(Can be prepared 1 day ahead. Keep chilled.)*

Mix broth, soy sauce and cornstarch in small bowl. Heat 1½ teaspoons oil in large nonstick skillet over high heat. Add half of steak and half of juices from dish and sauté until steak is brown, about 1 minute. Transfer mixture to plate. Repeat with 1½ teaspoons oil, steak and juices. Return all steak and juices to skillet. Add green onions and radishes and sauté 1 minute. Stir broth mixture, add to skillet and sauté just until steak is cooked through and sauce thickens, about 4 minutes. Transfer to plates and serve.

6 SERVINGS

NAME THAT STEAK

A steak is more than just a steak: It's a porterhouse, a filet mignon or a New York, to name just three different cuts. Here's a brief explanation of what's what, exactly.

◆ Porterhouse: This steak comes from the short loin section, close to the ribs in the middle of the back. It is a very large piece of meat that has three components: parts of the tenderloin, the bone, and parts of another, triangular section of meat.

◆ Filet Mignon: The tenderloin section of a porterhouse, cut away and served separately. It is the most tender cut of beef.

◆ New York: The triangular section of meat on a porterhouse, cut away and served separately. It may also be called a New York strip steak, Delmonico steak or shell steak.

◆ Rib Eye: A large, well-marbled steak that comes from the outer side of the rib.

◆ Flank Steak: A large piece of meat cut from the lower hindquarters. Usually served sliced.

◆ Top Round: Another large steak, from the inner portion of the hind leg. Often served sliced.

◆ ◆ ◆

Saffron is reputed to be worth its weight in gold. The main reason why this spice is so expensive—ranging from five to ten dollars per gram—is that the production of saffron is extremely labor intensive.

The vibrant orange-red saffron "threads," used in a variety of Mediterranean recipes, are really dried stigma sections of a certain type of crocus flower called *Crocus sativus*. Each flower has only three stigmas and, although the numbers vary, it can take upwards of 500 stigmas to make a single gram of saffron.

In addition, the threads must be picked by hand during a two-week period in autumn, the only time of the year when these flowers bloom.

Saffron's high price has lured less-than-honest merchants to dilute ground saffron with other fillers. The best way to guarantee that you are buying pure saffron is to purchase only whole threads. If a recipe calls for saffron powder, the threads can be ground with a mortar and pestle. On the bright side, it usually only takes a few saffron threads to fully flavor and color a big paella or risotto.

◆ ◆ ◆

Veal Scallops with Saffron and Porcini Mushrooms

◆ ◆ ◆

1¼ cups canned low-salt chicken broth
¾ ounce dried porcini mushrooms*

10 ounces veal scallops
All purpose flour
1 tablespoon butter
2 tablespoons olive oil
¼ cup finely chopped shallots
¼ cup dry white wine
¼ teaspoon (packed) saffron threads

Bring broth to simmer in small saucepan. Remove from heat. Add mushrooms and soak in broth until softened, about 30 minutes. Drain mushrooms; reserve soaking liquid. Coarsely chop.

Sprinkle veal with salt and pepper. Dredge veal in flour to coat; shake off excess. Melt butter with oil in heavy large skillet over medium-high heat. Add veal and sauté until brown, about 2 minutes per side. Transfer veal to plate; tent with foil to keep warm. Add shallots to same skillet and sauté until tender, about 2 minutes. Add mushrooms, reserved soaking liquid (leave any sediment in bowl), wine and saffron to skillet. Boil until reduced to sauce consistency, stirring occasionally, about 8 minutes. Season with salt and pepper. Spoon sauce over veal and then serve.

Porcini are available at Italian markets, specialty foods stores and many supermarkets.

2 SERVINGS

Curried Veal with Shallot and Pear Sauce

◆ ◆ ◆

9 ounces ¼-inch-thick veal scallops
1½ tablespoons butter
1 large pear, peeled, cored, coarsely chopped
¼ cup finely chopped shallots

1 teaspoon curry powder
½ cup dry white wine
⅓ cup whipping cream

Sprinkle veal with salt and pepper. Melt 1 tablespoon butter in heavy large skillet over medium-high heat. Add veal; sauté until just cooked through, about 1 minute per side. Transfer veal to plate. Add pear, shallots and remaining ½ tablespoon butter to same skillet. Cook until shallots are golden, about 2 minutes. Add curry powder; stir 1 minute. Add wine and cream and bring to boil. Reduce heat to medium; simmer until sauce thickens and pear is soft, about 3 minutes. Season with salt and pepper. Return veal and any accumulated juices to sauce. Simmer until just heated through, about 1 minute. Divide veal and sauce between plates; serve.

2 SERVINGS

Grilled Veal Chops with Rosemary

◆ ◆ ◆

5 tablespoons extra-virgin olive oil
¼ cup dry red wine
1½ tablespoons chopped fresh rosemary or 2 teaspoons dried
2 large garlic cloves, pressed
½ teaspoon salt
½ teaspoon ground black pepper
6 8-ounce veal rib chops (¾ to 1 inch thick)

Fresh rosemary sprigs

Whisk oil, wine, rosemary, garlic, salt and pepper to blend in 13 x 9 x 2-inch glass baking dish. Add veal chops to dish and turn to coat with marinade. Let stand at room temperature 1 hour or refrigerate up to 4 hours, turning veal occasionally.

Prepare barbecue (medium-high heat) or preheat broiler. Remove veal from marinade, shaking off excess. Season veal with salt and pepper. Lightly oil grill. Grill or broil veal to desired doneness, about 4 minutes per side for medium-rare. Transfer to platter. Garnish with rosemary sprigs and serve.

6 SERVINGS

◆ ◆ ◆

ITALIAN DINNER FOR SIX

PROSCIUTTO WITH MELON

GRILLED VEAL CHOPS WITH ROSEMARY
(AT LEFT; PICTURED ON PAGE 45)

POTATO AND PARMESAN GRATIN
(PAGE 147; PICTURED ON PAGE 44)

TOMATO SALAD
(PAGE 153; PICTURED ON PAGE 44)

SANGIOVESE DI ROMAGNA

RASPBERRY GRANITA
(PAGE 206)

PINE NUT CRESCENTS
(PAGE 217)

◆ ◆ ◆

Roast Veal Loin with Potatoes, Carrots and Squash

◆ ◆ ◆

1	3- to 3¼-pound boneless veal loin, tied
3	tablespoons plus ¾ teaspoon chopped fresh thyme
2	tablespoons plus ¼ teaspoon chopped fresh rosemary
5	tablespoons butter, room temperature
2¼	cups canned low-salt chicken broth
1	cup dry white wine
2	pounds baby red-skinned potatoes, halved
2	large onions, each cut lengthwise into 8 wedges
1½	pounds carrots, peeled, each cut crosswise into 4 pieces, then quartered lengthwise
1½	pounds assorted baby squash (such as pattypan and green and yellow zucchini)
3	tablespoons all purpose flour

Preheat oven to 350°F. Rub veal with 2 tablespoons thyme and 1 tablespoon rosemary; sprinkle veal with salt and pepper. Melt 2 tablespoons butter in heavy large skillet over medium-high heat. Add veal; sauté until brown on all sides, about 6 minutes. Transfer to large roasting pan. Add 1 cup broth and wine to same skillet; bring to boil, scraping up browned bits. Remove from heat.

Arrange potatoes, onions and carrots around veal in roasting pan. Sprinkle 1 tablespoon fresh thyme and 1 tablespoon fresh rosemary over vegetables. Pour broth-wine mixture over vegetables. Roast veal and vegetables until thermometer inserted into center of veal registers 145°F, about 50 minutes.

Transfer veal to platter; cover with foil. Increase oven temperature to 400°F. Add all squash to roasting pan; stir to mix with roasted vegetables. Cover pan with foil. Continue to roast until all vegetables are tender, about 20 minutes longer.

Using slotted spoon, arrange vegetables around veal. Cover with foil. Strain pan juices into medium saucepan. Add 1¼ cups broth, ¾ teaspoon thyme and ¼ teaspoon rosemary to saucepan. Mix flour and remaining 3 tablespoons butter in small bowl until well blended. Whisk into broth mixture. Boil over medium heat until gravy thickens, whisking constantly, about 4 minutes. Season with salt and pepper. Slice veal and serve with vegetables and gravy.

8 SERVINGS

◆ ◆ ◆

PARISIAN SUPPER FOR EIGHT

ASSORTED OLIVES AND CRUDITÉS

CRACKERS OR BAGUETTE SLICES`

VEGETABLE PÂTÉ

ROAST VEAL LOIN WITH POTATOES, CARROTS AND SQUASH (AT LEFT; PICTURED OPPOSITE)

DRY WHITE WINE

TOSSED SALAD

FRUIT TART

◆ ◆ ◆

Hazelnut-crusted Racks of Lamb with Tomato-Olive Ragout

◆ ◆ ◆

LAMB

1   cup plus 3 tablespoons olive oil

2   tablespoons chopped fresh rosemary

1   tablespoon chopped garlic

2   1⅓- to 1½-pound racks of lamb, backbones removed, trimmed, frenched

5   ounces egg bread, crusts trimmed, torn into pieces

½   cup chopped fresh parsley

¼   cup hazelnuts, toasted, husked

1   large shallot, quartered

TOMATO-OLIVE RAGOUT

1   tablespoon olive oil

16 ¾-inch-diameter pearl onions, blanched 30 seconds, peeled

1   tablespoon chopped garlic

½   teaspoon dried crushed red pepper

2   cups chopped fresh fennel bulb (about 1 large)

1	28-ounce can Italian-style tomatoes
½	cup brine-cured black olives (such as Kalamata), pitted, halved
3	tablespoons Dijon mustard
¼	cup chopped fresh basil
1	tablespoon butter

FOR LAMB: Mix 1 cup oil, rosemary and garlic in 13 x 9 x 2-inch glass baking dish. Sprinkle lamb with salt and pepper. Add to marinade and turn to coat on all sides. Cover and refrigerate overnight, turning occasionally.

Grind bread in processor until small crumbs form. Combine 2 cups crumbs (reserve any remaining crumbs for another use), parsley, nuts and shallot in processor. Process until nuts are finely ground. Gradually add 2 tablespoons oil; process until crumbs begin to stick together. Transfer to bowl. Season with salt and pepper. Add remaining 1 tablespoon oil; toss gently to coat. *(Coating can be made 1 day ahead. Cover; chill.)*

FOR TOMATO-OLIVE RAGOUT: Heat olive oil in heavy large skillet over medium-low heat. Add onions, garlic and dried red pepper. Sauté 5 minutes. Add fennel and sauté until translucent, about 3 minutes. Add tomatoes with their juices and olives. Increase heat and bring to gentle boil. Cook until onions are very tender and juices thicken, stirring occasionally and breaking up tomatoes with spoon, about 18 minutes. *(Can be prepared 1 day ahead. Cover; chill. Rewarm over medium heat before continuing.)*

Preheat oven to 400°F. Heat heavy large skillet over high heat. Remove lamb from marinade. Add lamb to skillet with some marinade still coating lamb. Cook until brown, about 4 minutes per side. (If necessary, brown 1 rack at a time.) Using tongs, transfer lamb to baking sheet; cool 15 minutes. Spread 1½ tablespoons mustard over rounded side of each rack; firmly press half of breadcrumb coating into mustard on each rack.

Roast lamb until thermometer inserted into center registers 135°F for medium-rare, about 25 minutes. Let lamb rest 15 minutes.

Meanwhile, mix basil and butter into warm ragout; stir until butter melts. Season to taste with salt and pepper.

Transfer lamb to cutting board. Using large knife, cut lamb between bones into individual chops. Divide chops among 4 plates. Spoon ragout alongside chops and serve.

4 SERVINGS

Use a boning knife to trim any fat from the top of both lamb racks. Starting at one end, cut into the layer of fat; then hold the fat and pull it back as you cut it off.

A classic rack of lamb has the rib bones exposed. Use the boning knife to cut away approximately two inches of fat between the bones; this technique is called frenching.

To carve the rack, keep it steady by holding onto a bone. Use a large knife to cut the rack between the bones into individual chops.

Roast Lamb with Cherry Tomato and Arugula Salad

◆ ◆ ◆

1   5-pound leg of lamb, boned, butterflied, trimmed of excess fat
7   tablespoons extra-virgin olive oil
⅓   cup plus ¼ cup chopped mixed fresh herbs (such as oregano, rosemary, thyme and parsley)

3   tablespoons dry red wine

6   ounces fresh arugula
24 cherry tomatoes, halved
2   teaspoons fresh lemon juice

1   teaspoon grated lemon peel

The secret to this classic Italian dish is to rub the lamb with herbs at least 12 hours before cooking to bring out the best flavor. A simple salad made with peppery arugula and ripe cherry tomatoes is a terrific partner.

◆ ◆ ◆

Place lamb, boned side up, on baking sheet. Rub 2 tablespoons oil over lamb. Sprinkle with salt and pepper. Rub ⅓ cup herbs over lamb. Cover and refrigerate at least 12 hours or overnight.

Preheat oven to 400°F. Whisk 1 tablespoon oil, remaining ¼ cup herbs and red wine in medium bowl. Roast lamb 10 minutes. Pour red wine mixture over lamb. Roast lamb until thermometer inserted into thickest part registers 135°F for medium-rare, about 10 minutes longer. Transfer lamb and any pan juices to platter. Cover lamb with foil; let stand 10 minutes.

Meanwhile, arrange arugula on another platter. Top with

tomatoes. Sprinkle with salt and pepper. Whisk lemon juice and remaining 4 tablespoons oil in small bowl. Season to taste with salt and pepper. Drizzle half of oil mixture over salad.

Cut lamb on diagonal into thin slices. Return lamb to same platter. Add lemon peel to remaining oil mixture. Drizzle oil mixture over lamb. Serve with tomato and arugula salad.

6 SERVINGS

Olive-stuffed Leg of Lamb

◆ ◆ ◆

LAMB

1   cup dry white breadcrumbs
½   cup pitted brine-cured black olives (such as Kalamata)
¼   cup olive oil
3   tablespoons chopped fresh oregano
2   tablespoons chopped fresh marjoram
1½   tablespoons fresh thyme leaves
3   garlic cloves
2   anchovy fillets
1   7-pound leg of lamb, boned, butterflied

SAUCE

1   cup fresh lemon juice
½   cup olive oil
2   teaspoons dried thyme
1   teaspoon cayenne pepper

FOR LAMB: Preheat oven to 400°F. Blend first 8 ingredients in processor until paste forms. Open lamb, smooth side down, on large baking sheet. Spread paste over butterflied lamb. Starting at 1 long side, roll lamb up tightly and tie at several places with kitchen string to hold shape.

FOR SAUCE: Mix all ingredients in medium bowl to blend. Season sauce to taste with salt and pepper. Pour ¾ cup sauce into small bowl and set aside; reserve remainder.

Brush lamb with 2 tablespoons of remaining sauce in medium bowl. Roast lamb until meat thermometer inserted into center registers 140°F for medium-rare, basting occasionally with sauce in medium bowl, about 1 hour. Let stand 15 minutes.

Slice lamb and arrange on platter. Drizzle reserved ¾ cup sauce over sliced lamb and serve.

10 SERVINGS

WINE-TASTING DINNER FOR TEN

ROSEMARY BREAD WITH
FLAVORED OLIVE OILS

ROSÉ

OLIVE-STUFFED LEG OF LAMB
(AT LEFT; PICTURED ABOVE)

SWEET POTATO GRATIN
WITH GINGER
(PAGE 145; PICTURED ABOVE)

GREEN BEANS

BROILED TOMATOES

SYRAH

PEAR TART WITH
BUTTERSCOTCH SAUCE
(PAGE 178)

VIN SANTO

◆ ◆ ◆

Braised Lamb Shanks with Fresh Rosemary

◆ ◆ ◆

6	lamb shanks (about 5 pounds total)
2	tablespoons olive oil
2	medium onions, chopped
3	large carrots, peeled, cut into ¼-inch-thick rounds
10	garlic cloves, minced
1	750-ml bottle dry red wine
1	28-ounce can diced tomatoes with juices
1	14½-ounce can low-salt chicken broth
1	14½-ounce can beef broth
5	teaspoons chopped fresh rosemary
2	teaspoons chopped fresh thyme
2	teaspoons grated lemon peel

Sprinkle shanks with salt and pepper. Heat oil in heavy large pot over medium-high heat. Working in batches, add shanks to pot; cook until brown on all sides, about 8 minutes. Transfer to bowl.

Add onions, carrots and garlic to pot and sauté until golden, about 10 minutes. Stir in all remaining ingredients. Return shanks to pot, pressing down to submerge. Bring liquids to boil. Reduce heat to medium-low. Cover; simmer until meat is tender, about 2 hours.

Uncover pot; simmer until meat is very tender, about 30 minutes longer. *(Can be made 1 day ahead. Chill until cold; cover and keep chilled. Rewarm over medium heat before continuing.)* Transfer shanks to platter; tent with foil. Boil juices in pot until thickened, about 15 minutes. Season with salt and pepper. Spoon over shanks.

6 SERVINGS

Pan-fried Lamb Chops with Garlic

◆ ◆ ◆

2   tablespoons minced garlic
1½ tablespoons chopped fresh rosemary or 2 teaspoons dried
1   teaspoon dried crushed red pepper
18 small lamb rib chops

3   tablespoons olive oil
    Fresh rosemary sprigs

Combine first 3 ingredients in small bowl. Rub about ¼ tea-spoon mixture over both sides of each chop. Sprinkle chops with salt; place on plate. Cover; chill at least 30 minutes and up to 4 hours.

Heat 1½ tablespoons oil in heavy large skillet over medium heat. Add 9 chops to skillet; cook to desired doneness, about 3 minutes per side for medium-rare. Transfer to platter; cover with foil. Repeat with remaining oil and chops. Garnish platter with rosemary sprigs.

6 SERVINGS

Lamb Tikka with Crispy Onions

◆ ◆ ◆

⅓ cup plain low-fat yogurt
1   tablespoon minced peeled fresh ginger
1½ teaspoons curry powder
12 ounces trimmed boneless lamb sirloin chops, cut into 12 pieces

1   medium-size red onion, thinly sliced into rounds
2   teaspoons olive oil
2   bamboo skewers, soaked in water 30 minutes, drained
   Lemon wedges

Preheat broiler. Spray broiler pan with nonstick vegetable oil spray. Whisk yogurt, ginger and curry powder in medium bowl to blend. Season lamb pieces with salt and pepper. Stir into yogurt mixture and let stand 5 minutes.

Meanwhile, place onion rounds in shallow bowl. Sprinkle with salt and pepper. Drizzle with olive oil; toss to coat. Spread out onion in ½-inch-thick layer on broiler pan. Thread lamb pieces onto wooden skewers. Arrange skewers alongside onion.

Broil lamb and onion about 5 inches from heat source until lamb is brown outside but still pink inside and onion is lightly charred, turning occasionally, 10 minutes. Serve with lemon.

2 SERVINGS

◆ ◆ ◆

SATURDAY NIGHT DINNER FOR SIX

PAN-FRIED LAMB CHOPS
WITH GARLIC
(AT LEFT; PICTURED OPPOSITE)

MASHED POTATOES
WITH BLACK OLIVES
(PAGE 145; PICTURED OPPOSITE)

GREEN BEANS

MERLOT OR PINOT NOIR

LEMON CHEESECAKE
WITH HAZELNUT CRUST
(PAGE 188; PICTURED OPPOSITE)

◆ ◆ ◆

Pork Tenderloin with Ancho Chili Mole

◆ ◆ ◆

SAUCE

3   large dried ancho chilies,* wiped clean with damp paper towel

½   5- to 6-inch corn tortilla, torn into ½-inch pieces
2   tablespoons pine nuts
2   tablespoons sesame seeds

4   whole plum tomatoes
1   ½-inch-thick onion slice
2   large garlic cloves, unpeeled
1   2-inch piece cinnamon stick
3   whole cloves

1   cup canned low-salt chicken broth

2   tablespoons corn oil
1   tablespoon golden brown sugar
1   teaspoon unsweetened cocoa powder
1   tablespoon Sherry wine vinegar

PORK

2   12-ounce pork tenderloins
1½   tablespoons corn oil
1½   tablespoons chopped fresh marjoram

FOR SAUCE: Place chilies in heavy medium skillet over medium heat. Toast until darker in color and fragrant, turning often with tongs, about 6 minutes. Transfer to large plate.

Add tortilla, pine nuts and sesame seeds to same skillet. Stir over medium heat until tortilla is pale brown, nuts are toasted and seeds are deep golden, about 4 minutes. Transfer to same plate.

Add tomatoes, onion, garlic, cinnamon and cloves to skillet. Toast cinnamon and cloves until fragrant and beginning to darken, about 7 minutes; transfer to same plate. Toast tomatoes, onion and garlic until slightly charred and tender, turning often, about 8 minutes longer; transfer to same plate. Set skillet aside to use later.

Cut stems off chilies. Cut chilies open. Scrape out seeds and discard. Tear chilies into small pieces. Peel and core tomatoes; peel garlic.

Many of the ingredients for the sauce are toasted in a dry skillet before they are pureed. This technique heightens their flavor and adds a smoky nuance to the sauce. First, toast the chilies over medium heat, turning them often, until they become darker and fragrant.

Toasting the whole tomatoes, onion slice, garlic and spices in the skillet provides those ingredients with the charred, fire-roasted taste of foods cooked over an open grill.

Errata: This is the correct text for the
Pork Tenderloin with Ancho Chili Mole on page 69.

Puree chilies and broth in blender until only tiny bits of chilies remain, about 4 minutes. Add tomatoes, onion, garlic, cinnamon and cloves; puree until smooth. Add tortilla, pine nuts and sesame seeds; puree until sauce is smooth and thick.

Heat oil in same skillet over medium-high heat. Add sauce from blender, sugar and cocoa; whisk to blend. Simmer 3 minutes. Whisk in vinegar. Season with salt and pepper. *(Sauce can be prepared 4 days ahead. Let cool. Transfer to container; cover and chill.)*

FOR PORK: Place pork in glass baking dish. Drizzle oil over; sprinkle with marjoram, salt and pepper. Turn pork to coat evenly. Marinate at room temperature 1 hour or cover and chill 1 day.

Preheat oven to 375°F. Heat large ovenproof skillet over medium-high heat. Add pork tenderloins and brown on all sides, about 5 minutes. Transfer skillet to oven. Roast pork until thermometer inserted into thickest part registers 155°F, about 15 minutes. Transfer pork to platter; let rest 5 minutes.

Meanwhile, rewarm sauce over low heat, stirring frequently.

Cut pork crosswise into ½-inch-thick slices. Arrange on platter. Spoon sauce over pork and serve immediately.

*Available in Latin American markets and some supermarkets.

4 SERVINGS

To seed the chilies, cut them open lengthwise; shake out the loose seeds, and scrape out the remaining seeds with a small knife.

Pan-Asian Teriyaki Spareribs

◆ ◆ ◆

2   3-pound racks pork spareribs, trimmed

1   12-ounce bottle thick teriyaki baste and glaze
⅓   cup dry Sherry
4   teaspoons dark brown sugar
1   tablespoon finely chopped peeled fresh ginger
1½   teaspoons chili-garlic sauce*

1   cup hickory smoke chips, soaked in water 30 minutes, drained

Position rack in middle of oven and preheat to 375°F. Sprinkle ribs with pepper. Wrap each rib rack tightly with heavy-duty foil. Set packets on large rimmed baking sheet. Bake ribs until just tender, about 1 hour 15 minutes. Cool ribs 30 minutes in foil. Unwrap foil. Pour all juices from ribs into medium bowl. *(Can be made 1 day ahead. Cover ribs and pan juices separately and chill.)*

Spoon off and discard fat from surface of pan juices. Stir teriyaki baste and next 4 ingredients into pan juices.

Prepare barbecue (medium heat). Place chips in 8 x 6-inch foil packet with open top. Set packet atop coals about 5 minutes before grilling. Grill ribs until heated through and well glazed, turning and basting often with teriyaki mixture, about 20 minutes.

Available in the Asian foods section of many supermarkets.

4 SERVINGS

Pork and Chipotle Tacos

◆ ◆ ◆

1   2½-pound bone-in pork butt

2   tablespoons corn oil
2   large onions, chopped
1½   cups chopped fresh cilantro
3   tablespoons chopped canned chipotle chilies*

12   5- to 6-inch-diameter corn tortillas
2   15- to 16-ounce cans black beans, rinsed, drained

1½   cups chopped green onions
2   avocados, pitted, peeled, diced
    Purchased tomatillo salsa
    Lime wedges

Preheat oven to 350°F. Place pork on baking sheet and sprinkle with salt and pepper. Roast pork until brown and very tender, about 2 hours. Cool. Shred pork.

Heat oil in large skillet over medium-high heat. Add onions; sauté until tender, 10 minutes. Add pork, cilantro and chilies with sauce; stir until heated. Season with salt and pepper.

Preheat oven to 350°F. Wrap tortillas in foil. Heat in oven 10 minutes. Stir beans in saucepan over medium-low heat until heated through. Coarsely mash beans.

Arrange tortillas on work surface. Spread mashed beans over. Top with pork mixture. Sprinkle with green onions and avocados. Serve with tomatillo salsa and lime wedges.

Available at Latin American markets and some supermarkets.

4 SERVINGS

Pork Chops with Mango-Basil Sauce

◆ ◆ ◆

1	small mango, peeled, pitted
1	tablespoon plus 2 teaspoons vegetable oil
1	tablespoon minced garlic
1	jalapeño chili, seeded, minced
⅓	cup thinly sliced fresh basil leaves
¾	cup canned low-salt chicken broth
1½	tablespoons golden brown sugar
1	tablespoon soy sauce
4	6- to 8-ounce center-cut pork chops (about 1 inch thick)

Puree mango in processor. Set aside ½ cup puree.

Heat 1 tablespoon oil in medium skillet over medium heat. Add garlic and jalapeño, then basil; sauté just until basil wilts, about 1 minute. Add broth, brown sugar and soy sauce. Bring to boil, stirring occasionally. Reduce heat to low and simmer 3 minutes. Gradually whisk in ½ cup mango puree. Simmer until sauce thickens and coats spoon, about 5 minutes. Season with salt and pepper.

Prepare barbecue or preheat broiler. Brush pork with 2 teaspoons oil. Sprinkle with salt and pepper. Grill or broil pork until just cooked through, about 5 minutes per side. Transfer to plates.

Rewarm sauce over low heat. Drizzle over pork.

4 SERVINGS

ABOUT MANGOES

Not too long ago, mangoes were exotic fare; now they can be found nationwide and on menus from California to Connecticut. And it's no wonder that mangoes have caught on: With their luscious texture and sweet peachy taste, they are ideal eaten fresh or used in a variety of recipes.

When selecting a mango for eating or cooking, look for one with a crimson blush and a musky perfume. If it does not yield when gently pressed, let it ripen at room temperature for several days. Keep a ripe mango chilled.

Unlike most other fruits, the flesh of a mango clings very tightly to the flat pit that runs almost its entire length, so pitting a mango can be tricky. Begin by peeling it with a paring knife. Cut a small slice off the stem end, then stand the mango on its cut end, with one narrow side facing you. Cutting vertically about one-half inch from the center, remove one side of the fruit from the pit. Repeat on the other side. Then cut off the remaining flesh around the pit.

◆ ◆ ◆

Cumin Pork Roast with Wild Mushroom Sauce

1	3½-pound center-cut pork loin
4	teaspoons ground cumin
3	tablespoons butter
14	ounces oyster mushrooms, halved
½	cup plus 1 tablespoon chopped shallots
2	tablespoons finely chopped garlic
1	tablespoon plus 1 teaspoon finely chopped jalapeño chili (with seeds)
2	tablespoons finely chopped fresh cilantro
2	tablespoons finely chopped fresh oregano
1	14½-ounce can low-salt chicken broth
2	tablespoons all purpose flour
¼	cup dry Sherry
	Cilantro sprigs ◆ ◆ ◆

Preheat oven to 375°F. Sprinkle pork with salt and pepper. Rub 3 teaspoons cumin over pork. Place in roasting pan. Roast pork until thermometer inserted into center registers 150°F, about 50 minutes.

Meanwhile, melt 2 tablespoons butter in large skillet over medium-high heat. Add mushrooms, ½ cup shallots, garlic and 1 tablespoon jalapeño; sauté until mushrooms are very tender and beginning to brown, about 15 minutes. Remove from heat. Add chopped cilantro, oregano and 1 teaspoon cumin. Season mushroom mixture to taste with salt and pepper. Set aside.

Transfer pork to platter. Tent with foil. Add broth to roasting pan; scrape up any browned bits. Transfer to heavy medium saucepan. Gradually whisk flour into Sherry in medium bowl to blend. Whisk Sherry mixture, 1 tablespoon butter, 1 tablespoon shallots and 1 teaspoon jalapeño into broth; bring to boil, whisking until smooth. Stir in mushroom mixture and any accumulated juices from pork on platter. Boil until mixture thickens to sauce consistency, stirring occasionally, about 5 minutes. Season with salt and pepper.

Slice pork. Garnish with cilantro sprigs; serve with sauce.

8 SERVINGS

A LITTLE LEFTOVER

One of the best things about a roast is that the leftovers can easily become another meal. Here are some ideas for reviving the pork roast at left (pictured opposite with Spinach-Orange Salad, page 154; Mashed Potatoes with Cilantro and Roasted Chilies, page 146; and Coffee Ice Cream Sundaes with Pine Nut-Caramel Sauce, page 209), courtesy of Jeanne Thiel Kelley, a contributor to *Bon Appétit*.

◆ Pork and Mushroom Burritos: Chop the pork and mix it with any leftover mashed potatoes and mushroom sauce. Roll this mixture up in burrito-size flour tortillas, and transfer to a baking dish. Cover with grated Jack cheese and bake until cheese melts and burritos are warm. Sprinkle with chopped tomatoes and green onions.

◆ Pork and Potato Hash: Sauté chopped onions. Add parboiled cubed potatoes and sauté, then cubed pork, remaining mushroom sauce and chicken broth to moisten. Serve with corn bread.

◆ Southwestern Shepherd's Pie: Mix canned black beans, cubed pork, defrosted corn kernels and chicken broth to moisten. Transfer to casserole. Top with mashed potatoes and Jack cheese and bake until warm.

◆ ◆ ◆

Roasted Chicken Sandwiches with Jack Cheese and Chili Mayonnaise

◆ ◆ ◆

1½ cups mayonnaise
3 large garlic cloves, minced
2 teaspoons minced canned chipotle chilies*

1 large red bell pepper
1 large yellow bell pepper
1 large orange bell pepper
5 cups mixed baby greens
5 medium tomatoes, thinly sliced

12 6- to 8-ounce skinless boneless chicken breast halves
2 tablespoons olive oil
12 ounces Monterey Jack cheese with jalapeños, sliced

4 French bread baguettes, ends trimmed, each cut crosswise into 3 equal pieces, halved lengthwise

Mix mayonnaise, garlic and chipotle chilies in medium bowl. Season with salt and pepper. Transfer to serving bowl.

Char bell peppers over gas flame or in broiler until blackened on all sides. Place in bag; let stand 10 minutes. Peel; seed. Cut into 1-inch-wide strips. *(Mayonnaise and peppers can be prepared 1 day ahead. Cover separately; refrigerate.)* Arrange peppers on platter with mixed baby greens and sliced tomatoes.

Preheat oven to 400°F. Lightly oil heavy large baking sheet. Place chicken on baking sheet. Brush chicken with oil. Sprinkle with salt and pepper. Bake until cooked through, about 10 minutes. Transfer chicken to cutting board. Cut crosswise into ½-inch-wide slices, keeping slices of each breast together. Return to baking sheet. Top with cheese. Bake until cheese melts, about 2 minutes.

Transfer chicken to platter and serve with bread, mayonnaise, roasted bell peppers, mixed greens and tomatoes.

Chipotle chilies canned in a spicy tomato sauce are available at Latin American markets and some supermarkets.

12 SERVINGS

Maple-Mustard Chicken

◆ ◆ ◆

3   tablespoons olive oil
2   large garlic cloves, minced
2   tablespoons chopped fresh rosemary or 2 teaspoons dried
2   tablespoons chopped fresh chives
2   tablespoons apple cider vinegar
⅓   cup pure maple syrup
¼   cup spicy brown mustard (such as Gulden's)
6   skinless boneless chicken breast halves

Fresh rosemary sprigs (optional)

Heat 2 tablespoons oil in heavy large skillet over medium heat. Add garlic; sauté 30 seconds. Add chopped herbs and vinegar; cook 30 seconds. Pour into bowl; cool. Whisk in syrup and mustard. Place chicken in glass baking dish. Pour marinade over; turn to coat. Sprinkle with pepper. Cover; chill at least 1 hour or overnight.

Heat 1 tablespoon oil in heavy large nonstick skillet over medium-high heat. Remove chicken from marinade. Sprinkle with salt and pepper. Add to skillet and sauté 2 minutes per side. Reduce heat to medium. Continue cooking until chicken is cooked through and brown, about 3 minutes per side. Transfer to platter.

Garnish with rosemary, if desired.

6 SERVINGS

Chicken Brochettes with Red Bell Peppers and Feta

◆ ◆ ◆

1	cup plain nonfat yogurt
5	tablespoons (packed) crumbled feta cheese
2	teaspoons minced garlic
1	teaspoon chopped fresh rosemary
¼	teaspoon pepper
1½	pounds skinless boneless chicken breasts, cut into 1½-inch pieces
2	large red bell peppers, cut into 1½-inch pieces
6	10- to 12-inch-long wooden skewers, soaked in water 30 minutes

Mix yogurt, 3 tablespoons feta cheese, garlic, rosemary and pepper in large bowl. Add chicken and toss to coat. Let chicken marinate at room temperature 30 minutes.

Prepare barbecue (medium-high heat) or preheat broiler. Thread chicken and red bell pepper pieces alternately onto skewers. Sprinkle with salt and pepper. Grill or broil until chicken is cooked through, turning occasionally, about 8 minutes.

Transfer chicken brochettes to platter. Sprinkle with remaining 2 tablespoons feta cheese and serve.

6 SERVINGS

Mojo is a tart Cuban sauce made of cumin, garlic and citrus juices. It's added to sandwiches, vegetables, grilled fish and meats. Here, mojo becomes the marinade for chicken in a tasty main-course salad.

Cuban-Style Grilled Mojo Chicken with Avocados and Mangoes

◆ ◆ ◆

DRESSING

1	cup plus 2 tablespoons vegetable oil
¾	cup orange juice
1	tablespoon (packed) grated orange peel
1	tablespoon honey
1	tablespoon soy sauce

CHICKEN

2	teaspoons cumin seeds
6	large garlic cloves, minced
1	large serrano chili, stemmed, minced
½	teaspoon salt
¾	cup olive oil
3	tablespoons orange juice
3	tablespoons fresh lime juice
6	skinless boneless chicken breast halves
2	large firm but ripe mangoes, peeled, pitted, cut into ½-inch pieces
2	large avocados, peeled, pitted, cut into ½-inch pieces
10	ounces mixed baby lettuces
¾	cup roasted salted cashews

FOR DRESSING: Whisk oil, orange juice, peel, honey and soy sauce in small bowl. Season dressing to taste with salt and pepper.

FOR CHICKEN: Stir cumin seeds in heavy medium skillet over medium-high heat until seeds are fragrant and slightly darker in color, about 2 minutes. Transfer seeds to medium bowl. Add minced garlic, minced chili and salt to seeds; mash mixture with back of fork to form coarse paste. Heat olive oil in same skillet over medium-high heat until very hot, about 2 minutes. Pour hot olive oil over garlic mixture; stir to blend. Let stand 15 minutes. Whisk in orange juice and lime juice. Pour marinade into 13 x 9 x 2-inch glass baking dish and cool. Add chicken to marinade; turn to coat. Cover chicken and refrigerate at least 1 hour and up to 3 hours.

Combine mangoes and avocados in medium bowl. Add 6 tablespoons dressing and toss to coat.

Prepare barbecue (medium-high heat). Remove chicken from marinade; discard marinade. Grill chicken until cooked through, about 5 minutes per side. Transfer chicken to work surface. Let stand 5 minutes. Cut chicken crosswise into ⅓-inch-thick slices.

Place lettuces in large bowl. Toss with enough dressing to coat thoroughly. Mound on 6 plates. Arrange chicken atop lettuces on each plate. Spoon mangoes and avocados alongside. Sprinkle salads with cashews. Serve, passing remaining dressing separately.

6 SERVINGS

Creole Chicken and Okra Gumbo

◆ ◆ ◆

2   tablespoons vegetable oil
2   tablespoons all purpose flour
1   cup sliced frozen whole okra
1   14½-ounce can low-salt chicken broth
1   14½-ounce can diced tomatoes in juice
½   pound skinless boneless chicken thighs, cut into 1-inch pieces
1   teaspoon dried thyme
¾   to 1 teaspoon hot pepper sauce (such as Tabasco)

Stir oil and flour in large saucepan over high heat until smooth and dark brown, about 3 minutes. Mix in okra, then chicken broth and tomatoes with their juices; simmer 3 minutes. Sprinkle chicken with thyme, salt and pepper. Add to saucepan. Simmer gumbo uncovered until chicken is cooked through, about 10 minutes. Season gumbo with hot pepper sauce, salt and pepper and serve.

2 SERVINGS

CAJUN AND CREOLE

Risotto is Italian. Coq au Vin is French. Gumbo is Cajun—or is it Creole? The Cajun and Creole cooking styles are often confused, and it's easy to see why. Both cuisines, which evolved in the American South in the late eighteenth century, combine classical French cooking techniques with Spanish, Italian and Native American influences. Both make use of some of the same ingredients, such as filé powder (a seasoning made from crushed sassafrass leaves). To complicate matters further, both Cajun and Creole cooks often claim dishes like gumbo and jambalaya as their own.

The most obvious difference between the two styles is that Cajun is considered country food while Creole is city food. When the Cajuns settled in the southern Louisiana bayou country, they cooked whatever they could find from the local fields, forests and waters. This improvisational aspect of their cooking is one of the hallmarks of Cajun cuisine.

Creole food tends to be more sophisticated than its down-home counterpart. Creole cooks are more likely to use butter or cream instead of rendered fat (a Cajun staple) and to use relatively extravagant ingredients (like fresh shellfish).

◆ ◆ ◆

SUNDAY NIGHT SUPPER FOR FOUR

CHICKEN AND VEGETABLE SAUTÉ
OVER HERBED POLENTA
TRIANGLES
(AT RIGHT; PICTURED AT RIGHT)

RADICCHIO AND ARUGULA SALAD

PINOT GRIGIO

PEARS POACHED IN RED WINE,
CARDAMOM AND ORANGE
(PAGE 184)

◆ ◆ ◆

Chicken and Vegetable Sauté over Herbed Polenta Triangles

◆ ◆ ◆

2½   cups canned low-salt chicken broth
1½   teaspoons fennel seeds, crushed
½   teaspoon dried crushed red pepper
5   tablespoons olive oil
1   cup sliced onion
1   large red bell pepper, cut into strips
6   small yellow crookneck squash, cut into ¼-inch-thick slices
     (about 5 cups)

4   tablespoons all purpose flour
1   pound skinless boneless chicken breast halves,
     cut crosswise into ⅓-inch-wide strips
½   cup thinly sliced fresh basil

6   tablespoons balsamic vinegar
1   teaspoon (packed) brown sugar
2   tablespoons (¼ stick) butter

     Herbed Polenta Triangles (see recipe opposite)

Boil broth in small saucepan until reduced to 1 cup, about 12 minutes. Remove from heat. Combine fennel seeds and crushed red pepper in small bowl. Heat 2 tablespoons oil in heavy large skillet over medium-high heat. Add onion and bell pepper and sauté until golden and almost tender, about 4 minutes. Add squash and sauté until barely tender, about 2 minutes. Stir in half of fennel seed mixture. Season with salt and pepper. Transfer to large bowl.

Place 3 tablespoons flour in medium bowl. Add chicken and toss to coat with flour; shake off excess. Heat 3 tablespoons oil in same skillet over medium-high heat. Add chicken; stir just until cooked through, about 3 minutes. Stir in remaining fennel seed mixture. Return vegetables to skillet. *(Can be made 4 hours ahead. Cover and chill.)* Toss chicken and vegetables over medium-high heat until heated through. Season with salt and pepper. Mix in ¼ cup basil.

Mix vinegar and brown sugar in small skillet. Mix butter with remaining 1 tablespoon flour in small bowl. Bring vinegar mixture to boil. Add reduced broth and bring to boil. Whisk in butter mixture. Boil until sauce thickens slightly, whisking constantly, about 1 minute. Season sauce with salt and pepper.

Arrange 2 polenta triangles on each of 4 plates. Spoon chicken mixture over polenta triangles. Drizzle each with sauce. Garnish with remaining ¼ cup basil and serve.

4 SERVINGS

Herbed Polenta Triangles

Nonstick vegetable oil spray
2⅔ cups canned low-salt chicken broth
1½ tablespoons butter
¾ cup plus 2 tablespoons yellow cornmeal
2 tablespoons chopped Italian parsley
2 tablespoons chopped fresh basil

Spray 8 x 8 x 2-inch square glass baking dish with vegetable oil spray. Bring broth and butter to boil in heavy medium saucepan. Gradually add cornmeal, whisking constantly. Whisk until cornmeal mixture is very thick and starts pulling away from pan, about 6 minutes. Remove from heat. Stir in parsley and basil. Immediately transfer polenta to baking dish, spreading evenly. Cool 5 minutes, then cut polenta into 8 triangles; leave in baking dish. *(Can be prepared 1 day ahead. Cover and refrigerate. Rewarm polenta in microwave oven on high, about 2 minutes.)*

4 SERVINGS

ABOUT POLENTA

Once the "meat of the poor" in Italy, polenta has turned upscale in recent years, becoming a hot food on the urban American restaurant circuit. This comforting cornmeal porridge has also become popular in home kitchens, especially now that there's a pre-made version available in supermarkets across the country.

Sold in plastic-wrapped, sausage-shaped rolls, the new packaged polenta can be sliced into rounds and fried or loosened with water, broth or milk and heated to a soft, pudding consistency. When buying polenta logs, look for those that feel firm to the touch, with no evidence of water surrounding them.

Less ready-made but still low-maintenance is instant polenta, which comes dry in granular form. It cooks in just five to seven minutes.

Purists still make authentic polenta from scratch. Yellow cornmeal is added to simmering salted water and stirred every minute or two for at least half an hour and up to an hour. A less traditional but simpler method involves cooking the cornmeal in a double boiler. The gentler, more even heat means that the polenta requires stirring only every ten minutes or so.

◆ ◆ ◆

Chinese-flavored Fried Chicken with Green Onion-Ginger Dipping Sauce

◆ ◆ ◆

PICNIC BY THE LAKE FOR FOUR

CHINESE-FLAVORED
FRIED CHICKEN WITH GREEN
ONION-GINGER DIPPING SAUCE
(AT RIGHT; PICTURED ABOVE)

ASIAN SLAW WITH PEANUTS
(PAGE 158; PICTURED ABOVE)

SODAS OR BEER

LEMON-POPPY SEED
SANDWICH COOKIES
(PAGE 216)

◆ ◆ ◆

DIPPING SAUCE

½   cup soy sauce
½   cup thinly sliced green onions
2   tablespoons finely chopped fresh cilantro
1½   teaspoons finely chopped peeled fresh ginger
1½   teaspoons hot chili sesame oil*

CHICKEN

3   large eggs
2   tablespoons soy sauce
2   teaspoons oriental sesame oil
1   4- to 4¼-pound whole chicken, cut into 12 pieces

1   quart vegetable oil
1½   cups all purpose flour
3   tablespoons ground ginger
1   teaspoon salt
1   teaspoon ground pepper

2   1-inch pieces fresh ginger, halved lengthwise

FOR DIPPING SAUCE: Whisk all ingredients in small bowl to blend. *(Can be prepared 1 day ahead. Cover and refrigerate.)*

FOR CHICKEN: Whisk eggs, soy sauce and oriental sesame oil in large bowl to blend. Add chicken to egg mixture, turning to coat. Cover; refrigerate at least 2 hours or overnight.

Heat vegetable oil in heavy large pot over medium-high heat to 375°F. Mix flour, ground ginger, salt and pepper in bowl. Add chicken thighs and drumsticks to flour mixture; turn to coat.

Add fresh ginger to oil. Fry chicken thighs and drumsticks in hot oil until golden and cooked through, about 10 minutes per side. Using tongs, transfer chicken to paper towels; drain. Coat chicken breasts and wings with flour mixture. Fry until golden and cooked through, about 6 minutes per side. Transfer chicken to paper towels. *(Can be prepared 2 hours ahead. Let stand at room temperature.)* Serve with dipping sauce.

Sesame oil flavored with red chilies is available at Asian markets and in the Asian foods section of some supermarkets.

4 SERVINGS

Chicken with Tomatoes, Onions and Mushrooms

◆ ◆ ◆

1   3¾-pound chicken, cut into 10 pieces
¼   cup all purpose flour
2   tablespoons (¼ stick) butter
1   tablespoon olive oil
1   pound mushrooms, trimmed
2   cups chopped seeded tomatoes
1½   cups dry white wine
1   10-ounce container pearl onions, blanched 1 minute, peeled

     Chopped fresh Italian parsley

Sprinkle chicken with salt and pepper. Dredge in flour; shake off excess. Melt butter with oil in heavy large pot over medium-high heat. Working in batches, add chicken to pot; cook until golden on all sides, about 6 minutes total. Transfer to bowl. Add mushrooms to pot; sauté until golden, about 5 minutes. Stir in tomatoes, wine and onions. Return chicken and any accumulated juices to pot. Reduce heat to medium. Cover and simmer 20 minutes.

Uncover pot and simmer until chicken is cooked through, about 10 minutes longer. Season to taste with salt and pepper. Transfer to serving bowl. Sprinkle with parsley.

4 SERVINGS

◆ ◆ ◆

RUSTIC DINNER BY THE HEARTH FOR FOUR

GARLIC AND ANCHOVY DIP
WITH VEGETABLES
(PAGE 14)

CHICKEN WITH TOMATOES, ONION
AND MUSHROOMS
(AT LEFT; PICTURED AT LEFT)

SPINACH GNOCCHI WITH
FONTINA CHEESE
(PAGE 122)

CRUSTY BREAD

BARBARESCO

COFFEE GELATO AND BISCOTTI

◆ ◆ ◆

Roasted Red Curry Chicken with Apple Jus

◆ ◆ ◆

CHICKENS

3	tablespoons vegetable oil
2	tablespoons Thai red curry paste*
2	3½-pound whole chickens
1	Granny Smith apple, quartered
1	head of garlic, halved crosswise
8	fresh cilantro sprigs
8	fresh mint sprigs

JUS

1	teaspoon yellow mustard seeds
5	tablespoons butter
6	tablespoons chopped shallots
4	fresh thyme sprigs
1	teaspoon (packed) brown sugar
4	cups chicken stock or canned low-salt broth
2	cups apple juice
¼	cup dry white wine
2	cinnamon sticks
2	tablespoons apple cider vinegar

The term *jus* usually refers to the juice from cooked meat, but it can also apply to the juice pressed from raw fruit. Serve this dish with chutney and basmati rice, if you like.

◆ ◆ ◆

FOR CHICKENS: Position rack in center of oven and preheat to 350°F. Mix oil and curry paste in small bowl. Rinse chickens; pat dry. Sprinkle inside and out with salt and pepper. Place apple, garlic, cilantro and mint in cavities of chickens, dividing equally. Rub curry mixture over chickens. Tie legs together.

Place chickens in large roasting pan. Roast until meat thermometer inserted into thickest part of thigh registers 175°F, basting chickens occasionally, about 1 hour 15 minutes. Transfer chickens to platter. Tent chickens with foil.

MEANWHILE, PREPARE JUS: Shake mustard seeds in medium skillet over low heat until color darkens and seeds begin to pop, about 2 minutes. Transfer mustard seeds to medium bowl.

Melt 1 tablespoon butter in heavy large skillet over medium-high heat. Add shallots, thyme and brown sugar to skillet and sauté until shallots are translucent, about 3 minutes. Add chicken stock, apple juice, wine and cinnamon sticks. Boil until mixture is reduced to 1 cup, about 20 minutes. Strain into medium saucepan. Bring jus to simmer. Add apple cider vinegar, toasted mustard

seeds and remaining 4 tablespoons butter and whisk just until butter melts. Season with salt and pepper. Serve jus with chickens.

Thai red curry paste is available at Asian markets and in the Asian foods section of some supermarkets.

4 SERVINGS

Herb-roasted Chicken Breasts

◆ ◆ ◆

3	large garlic cloves, chopped
1	tablespoon chopped fresh rosemary or 1 teaspoon dried
1	tablespoon chopped fresh thyme or 1 teaspoon dried
6	large chicken breast halves with skin and bones
3	tablespoons olive oil
⅓	cup dry white wine

Preheat oven to 375°F. Combine garlic, rosemary and thyme in small bowl. Arrange chicken in large roasting pan. Sprinkle chicken with salt and pepper. Rub with garlic mixture; drizzle with olive oil. Pour wine into bottom of pan. Bake chicken until just cooked through, about 30 minutes. Remove from oven.

Preheat broiler. Broil chicken until skin browns, about 3 minutes. Transfer chicken to platter and serve.

6 SERVINGS

ALL ABOUT MUSTARD SEEDS

A key ingredient in pickles, a unique flavoring in vinegar and a welcome crunch in potato salad, mustard seeds have been part of the world's pantry for millennia. The Greeks and Romans used them, and some historians claim that the seeds were known in Africa and China even earlier, possibly in prehisotric times.

Reference to the spherical, pinhead-size seeds can also be found in Indian religious lore, and to this day, the seeds are vital to many of the country's cuisines. Most commonly, they are ground to make sauces or mixed into seasoning blends.

Mustard is grown in several Indian states, but the leading producer of the crop is Canada, which provides about 90 percent of the world's supply. In the United States, the primary growing region is North Dakota. Most of the crop in this country yields the pale buff-colored seeds referred to as yellow or white mustard and found in pickling spice. By the way, the plant that produces these seeds is not the same one that carpets hillsides in spring: It may be pretty, but its seeds aren't suitable for cooking.

◆ ◆ ◆

Chicken, Shrimp and Sausage Stew

1	pound andouille sausage,* cut into rounds
6	large chicken thighs (about 2¼ pounds)
3	cups chopped onions
2⅓	cups chopped green bell peppers
1¼	cups chopped red bell peppers
6	large garlic cloves, chopped
3	tablespoons chopped fresh oregano
2	tablespoons chopped fresh thyme
1	tablespoon paprika
1	28-ounce can diced tomatoes in juice
1	14½-ounce can low-salt chicken broth
1	cup dry white wine
¾	cup sliced pimiento-stuffed green olives
1	pound uncooked large shrimp, peeled, deveined

Sauté sausage in heavy large pot over medium heat until brown, about 4 minutes. Transfer to large bowl. Sprinkle chicken with salt and pepper. Add chicken to pot and cook until browned, about 3 minutes per side. Transfer chicken to bowl with sausage. Pour off all but 1 tablespoon pan drippings.

Add onions and bell peppers to pot; sauté until vegetables are tender and light golden brown, about 15 minutes. Add garlic, oregano, thyme and paprika; sauté 2 minutes. Return sausage, chicken and any accumulated juices to pot. Add tomatoes with juices, chicken broth and wine. Bring to boil. Reduce heat; cover and simmer until chicken is cooked through, about 25 minutes.

Uncover pot. Add olives and simmer until chicken is very tender and liquid is reduced to thin sauce consistency, about 40 minutes. Add shrimp and simmer just until cooked through, about 5 minutes longer. Season to taste with salt and pepper. *(Stew can be prepared 1 day ahead. Refrigerate until cold, then cover tightly and refrigerate. Before serving, rewarm over medium-low heat.)*

*A smoked pork and beef sausage, available at specialty foods stores. Hot links, smoked bratwurst, kielbasa or smoked Hungarian sausage can be substituted.

6 SERVINGS

MIDWEEK DINNER FOR FOUR

CHICKEN, SHRIMP AND
SAUSAGE STEW
(AT LEFT; PICTURED OPPOSITE)

CURLY ENDIVE WITH
TOASTED ALMOND DRESSING
(PAGE 156; PICTURED OPPOSITE)

CRUSTY BREAD

SAUVIGNON BLANC

FRUIT TART

CASSOULET, OLD AND NEW

Arguments persist over where to find the most authentic cassoulet, with three towns in southern France—Toulouse, Castelnaudary and Carcassonne—all laying claims.

The name *cassoulet* comes from the old word *cassole*, the glazed earthenware pot used for cooking this homey country stew. Traditionally, dried lima beans (and later, white beans), pork rinds, and herbs were simmered in this pot. Any combination of duck confit, mutton, goose and sausage was browned and added to the pot, followed by a gratin topping. The dish was then slow cooked until thick and creamy.

Today, few consciences can swallow an old-fashioned, fat-packed cassoulet. New, healthful versions are popping up everywhere. Lean bacon is taking the place of pork rinds and olive oil is substituting for pork and duck fat. Leaner cuts of lamb and pork are being used. Even the sausage is being swapped for lighter varieties, such as the low-fat turkey kielbasa in the recipe at right (pictured with the Green Bean Caesar Salad from page 155)—all in the name of a cassoulet for the nineties.

◆ ◆ ◆

Low-Fat Cassoulet with Turkey Sausage

◆ ◆ ◆

1	1½-pound eggplant, unpeeled, coarsely chopped
1	pound mushrooms, quartered
2	10-ounce packages red or white pearl onions, peeled
4	medium carrots, chopped
2	medium-size fresh fennel bulbs, trimmed, chopped
1	cup dry white wine
12	teaspoons chopped assorted fresh herbs (such as thyme, rosemary and Italian parsley)
6	large garlic cloves, minced
4	cups canned seasoned crushed tomatoes with roasted garlic
2	14½-ounce cans low-salt chicken broth
⅔	cup dried red or brown lentils
2	15-ounce cans small white beans
1	pound low-fat smoked turkey sausage, coarsely chopped
2½	cups fresh breadcrumbs made from nonfat multi-grain bread
6	tablespoons freshly grated Parmesan cheese

Spray heavy large pot with vegetable oil spray. Heat over medium-high heat. Spray eggplant and mushrooms with vegetable oil spray; add to pot. Sauté until eggplant is tender and mushrooms are brown, about 20 minutes. Add onions, carrots and fennel to pot. Sauté until carrots are almost tender, about 20 minutes. Add wine, 4 teaspoons herbs and garlic. Simmer until wine is absorbed, about

4 minutes. Add tomatoes, broth and lentils. Cover and simmer until lentils are just tender, about 20 minutes. Mix in beans with their liquid, sausage and 4 teaspoons herbs. Simmer until flavors blend but cassoulet is still juicy, about 4 minutes. Season with salt and pepper. *(Can be prepared 1 day ahead; refrigerate.)*

Preheat oven to 350°F. Divide cassoulet mixture among eight 2- to 3-cup individual ovenproof casseroles. Mix breadcrumbs, cheese and remaining 4 teaspoons herbs in small bowl to blend. Sprinkle crumb mixture atop cassoulets. Bake uncovered until filling bubbles and topping is crisp, about 30 minutes.

8 SERVINGS

Curried Turkey Burgers

◆ ◆ ◆

1	tablespoon mustard seeds
¼	cup unsweetened applesauce
1	tablespoon plus ¾ cup plain nonfat yogurt
5	tablespoons mango chutney, mashed if chunky
3¼	teaspoons curry powder
¾	teaspoon salt
¼	teaspoon cayenne pepper
1	pound extra-lean ground turkey breast meat
7	tablespoons chopped green onion tops
7	tablespoons chopped fresh mint
¼	cup chopped tart green apple
4	5- to 6-inch-diameter pita breads
	Chopped lettuce

Shake mustard seeds in medium skillet over low heat until seeds begin to pop, about 2 minutes. Transfer seeds to bowl. Mix in applesauce, 1 tablespoon yogurt, 2 tablespoons chutney, 2½ teaspoons curry powder, salt and cayenne. Mix in turkey, 4 tablespoons onion tops and 4 tablespoons mint. Shape into four ¾-inch-thick patties.

Mix chopped apple, remaining ¾ cup yogurt, 3 tablespoons chutney, ¾ teaspoon curry powder, 3 tablespoons onion tops and 3 tablespoons mint in small bowl.

Prepare barbecue (medium heat). Spray burgers with nonstick vegetable oil spray and grill until cooked through, about 5 minutes per side. Cut 1 end off each pita and fill with 1 burger, some lettuce and ¼ of yogurt-chutney mixture.

4 SERVINGS

ALL ABOUT CAYENNE

Cayenne is the most widely cultivated type of chili in the world. Known in the spice trade as the "ginnie pepper," it is long, thin and curved, with a slightly wrinkled skin. Rich and warm red in color, it packs a real punch in the heat department.

In cooking, the pepper is most commonly used dried and either ground or crushed (as red pepper flakes, to sprinkle onto pizza and such). If you can get past the heat (on a scale of 10, cayenne falls somewhere between 7 and 8), the pepper actually does have a flavor: pungent, tart and smoky. Once dried and ground, though, neither the fire nor the flavor lasts long. The best way to preserve both is by storing your jar of cayenne in a cool, dark place. Replace the jar every six months or so.

Modern chili experts believe that cayenne originated either in Central or South America, then found its way north and east to the Caribbean and New Orleans. Along the way—and on a path that ultimately took it around the world—the pepper excited palates, caused brows to perspire and altered cookery forever.

◆ ◆ ◆

Grilled Game Hen with Moroccan Spices

◆ ◆ ◆

½   teaspoon curry powder
½   teaspoon ground coriander
½   teaspoon ground cumin
¼   teaspoon cayenne pepper
2   teaspoons minced garlic, mashed to paste

1   large Cornish game hen (about 1½ pounds), quartered

Prepare barbecue (medium-high heat). Stir curry powder, coriander, cumin and cayenne in heavy small skillet over medium-low heat until fragrant, about 1 minute. Remove from heat. Add mashed garlic to skillet and mix into spices.

Using fingertips, loosen skin of game hen pieces. Rub spice paste onto meat under skin. Sprinkle pieces with salt and pepper.

Place hen pieces on grill. Cover with foil; grill 10 minutes. Uncover; turn pieces over. Cover; continue to grill until golden brown, cooked through and juices run clear when hen is pierced with small knife, turning occasionally, about 10 minutes for breast pieces and 15 minutes for leg-thigh pieces. Serve hot or at room temperature.

2 SERVINGS

Roasted Game Hen with Citrus-Clove Glaze

◆ ◆ ◆

1   lemon, very thinly sliced
1   1½- to 1¾-pound Cornish game hen, halved, backbone discarded

⅓   cup all-fruit orange marmalade
2   tablespoons fresh lemon juice
1½   tablespoons bourbon
½   teaspooon grated lemon peel
¼   teaspoon ground cloves

Preheat oven to 450°F. Arrange lemon slices on baking sheet in two 3 x 5-inch rectangles. Season hen halves with salt and pepper. Place halves, skin side up, atop rectangles. Roast 15 minutes.

Meanwhile, combine marmalade, lemon juice, bourbon, lemon peel and cloves in heavy small saucepan. Simmer over medium heat until glaze thickens slightly, about 4 minutes.

Brush hen halves with glaze. Continue to roast until juices run clear when thighs are pierced and hen halves are deep brown, brushing 2 more times with glaze, about 10 minutes longer.

2 SERVINGS

◆ ◆ ◆

WEEKNIGHT DINNER FOR TWO

PLUM TOMATO SALAD

ROASTED GAME HEN WITH
CITRUS-CLOVE GLAZE
(AT LEFT; PICTURED LEFT)

BROCCOLI AND SUMMER SQUASH

CHARDONNAY

DOUBLE-NUT MAPLE BARS
(PAGE 215)

◆ ◆ ◆

Grilled Swordfish with Avocado Mayonnaise

◆ ◆ ◆

SOUTHWESTERN DINNER FOR SIX

SALSA AND TORTILA CHIPS

GRILLED SWORDFISH WITH
AVOCADO MAYONNAISE
(AT RIGHT; PICTURED OPPOSITE)

JICAMA AND GRILLED
RED PEPPER SLAW
(PAGE 156; PICTURED OPPOSITE)

BEER

GRILLED PINEAPPLE WITH
ICE CREAM

◆ ◆ ◆

AVOCADO MAYONNAISE

1½	large avocados, pitted, quartered
5	tablespoons mayonnaise
1	tablespoon fresh lime juice
¾	teaspoon hot pepper sauce (such as Tabasco)

SWORDFISH

1	cup thinly sliced green onions
¾	cup (packed) cilantro leaves
3	tablespoons extra-virgin olive oil
3	tablespoons fresh lime juice
1½	tablespoons grated lime peel
1½	tablespoons golden brown sugar
1	tablespoon coarsely chopped seeded jalapeño chili
6	8-ounce swordfish steaks (about ¾ inch thick)
1	cup hickory smoke chips, soaked in water 30 minutes, drained

FOR AVOCADO MAYONNAISE: Puree all ingredients in blender, scraping down sides occasionally. Season with salt and pepper. *(Can be made 4 hours ahead. Cover; chill.)*

FOR SWORDFISH: Blend first 7 ingredients in processor until almost smooth. Season to taste with salt and pepper. Pour marinade into 13 x 9 x 2-inch glass baking dish. Add swordfish, turning to coat. Cover and refrigerate 2 hours, or let stand at room temperature 1 hour, turning fish occasionally.

Prepare barbecue (medium heat). Place hickory smoke chips in 8 x 6-inch foil packet with open top. Set packet atop coals about 5 minutes before grilling. Grill fish until cooked through, basting often with marinade, about 4 minutes per side.

Serve swordfish with avocado mayonnaise.

6 SERVINGS

Grilled Spice-rubbed Salmon with Corn Salsa

◆ ◆ ◆

BARBECUE BY THE LAKE FOR TWELVE

TOMATO AND MOZZARELLA
BRUSCHETTA
(PAGE 25)

MIXED DRINKS

GRILLED SPICE-RUBBED SALMON
WITH CORN SALSA
(AT RIGHT; PICTURED AT RIGHT)

GREEN BEANS WITH
TOASTED PINE NUT OIL
(PAGE 141)

COUSCOUS

SAUVIGNON BLANC

FUDGY CHOCOLATE-
RASPBERRY BARS
(PAGE 214)

◆ ◆ ◆

SALMON

1½ tablespoons coriander seeds
1½ tablespoons mustard seeds
1½ tablespoons cumin seeds
1 teaspoon black peppercorns
3 tablespoons (packed) brown sugar

1 4-pound boneless side of salmon with skin

SALSA

6 cups fresh corn kernels (from about 9 ears) or frozen, thawed
1 cup finely chopped red onion
½ cup olive oil
½ cup chopped fresh cilantro
¼ cup fresh lime juice
1½ tablespoons minced seeded jalapeño chili

FOR SALMON: Heat heavy small skillet over medium-high heat. Add coriander, mustard and cumin seeds; sauté until fragrant, about 3 minutes. Add black peppercorns. Remove from heat and

cool. Finely grind mixture in spice grinder or in mortar with pestle. Transfer spice mixture to bowl. Mix in sugar.

Place salmon, skin side down, on large baking sheet. Rub ¼ cup spice mixture over salmon, pressing gently to adhere. Cover salmon with plastic and refrigerate at least 1 hour or overnight. Cover remaining spice mixture and let stand at room temperature.

FOR SALSA: Cook corn in saucepan of boiling salted water until just tender, about 2 minutes. Drain. Transfer to large bowl. Mix in remaining ingredients and 2 tablespoons spice mixture (reserve remaining spice mixture for another use). Season with salt. Cover and chill at least 1 hour or up to 4 hours before serving.

Prepare barbecue (medium heat). Grill salmon, skin side down, 6 minutes. Turn salmon over; grill until opaque in center, about 6 minutes more. Transfer salmon to platter. Serve with salsa.

12 SERVINGS

The simplest way to grill a side of salmon, as called for here, is to use a metal fish basket, a barbecue gadget that makes turning the fish easy. If you don't have one of these special baskets, cut the fish crosswise in half, and grill it in two pieces. Reassemble the fish on a platter, and top the cut area with some salsa.

Pan-fried Trout with Green Onions

◆ ◆ ◆

2	whole 11- to 12-ounce trout, boned or 4 fillets
	All purpose flour
1	tablespoon olive oil
3	green onions, chopped
½	cup dry white wine
1	tablespoon butter

Open each trout flat like a book. Sprinkle generously with salt and pepper. Dust trout with flour and shake off excess. Heat ½ tablespoon olive oil in heavy large skillet over medium-high heat. Add 1 trout and sauté until coating is crisp and trout is just opaque in center, about 2 minutes per side. Transfer trout to plate and tent with foil to keep warm. Repeat with remaining ½ tablespoon oil and trout.

Wipe out skillet with paper towels. Set aside 2 tablespoons green onions. Add remaining green onions, wine and butter to same skillet. Simmer over medium heat until mixture is almost reduced to glaze, stirring occasionally, about 3 minutes. Spoon sauce over trout. Sprinkle trout with reserved 2 tablespoons green onions.

2 SERVINGS

Roasted Salmon with Salsa Verde

◆ ◆ ◆

SALMON

1   9½-pound whole salmon without head, cleaned, scaled
    Nonstick vegetable oil spray
1   lemon, cut into ¼-inch-thick slices
12 sprigs mixed fresh herbs (such as parsley, thyme and oregano)
3   tablespoons extra-virgin olive oil

SALSA VERDE

3   cups chopped fresh parsley
2¼   cups extra-virgin olive oil
1   cup chopped green onion tops
¾   cup drained capers, chopped
½   cup fresh lemon juice
3   tablespoons minced garlic
1   tablespoon chopped fresh thyme
1   tablespoon chopped fresh oregano
1½   teaspoons chopped fresh rosemary
1½   teaspoons chopped fresh sage

     Dill sprigs
     Lemon slices

FOR SALMON: Preheat oven to 350°F. Pat salmon dry inside and out with paper towels. Sprinkle inside and out with salt and pepper. Center 36 x 18-inch heavy-duty foil sheet over heavy large baking sheet. Spray foil with oil spray. Place salmon diagonally on foil. Stuff with lemon and herb sprigs. Close salmon opening. Drizzle oil over salmon. Spray another sheet of foil with oil spray. Place foil sprayed side down over salmon. Crimp edges together to seal.

Bake salmon until meat thermometer inserted into thickest part of salmon registers 150°F, about 1½ hours. Remove top sheet of foil. Spoon all juices from salmon into small saucepan. Peel off skin from top of salmon. Scrape off any dark salmon meat. Let salmon cool 1 hour at room temperature. Boil reserved salmon juice until reduced to ½ cup, about 4 minutes. Cool. Cover salmon and reduced salmon juice separately and refrigerate overnight.

FOR SALSA VERDE: Mix first 10 ingredients and salmon juice in large bowl. Season with salt and pepper.

Place platter atop salmon. Invert salmon onto platter. Remove foil. Peel off skin. Scrape off any dark meat. Garnish with dill and lemon. Serve with salsa verde.

20 SERVINGS

Broiled Shark with Pesto Trapanese

♦ ♦ ♦

4   garlic cloves
25   large fresh basil leaves
¼   cup whole almonds, toasted
¾   pound plum tomatoes, peeled, seeded, chopped, drained
3   tablespoons extra-virgin olive oil
2   tablespoons chopped pitted imported green olives

4   5-ounce shark or swordfish steaks (about ¾ inch thick)
4   tablespoons dry white breadcrumbs

With processor running, drop garlic through feed tube; process until chopped. Scrape down sides of bowl. Add basil and almonds; chop finely. Add tomatoes, oil and olives; process using on/off turns until mixture resembles coarse paste (do not puree). Season with salt and pepper. *(Pesto can be prepared up to 4 hours ahead. Cover with plastic wrap and refrigerate.)*

Preheat oven to 400°F. Lightly oil large baking sheet. Arrange steaks on sheet. Sprinkle with salt and pepper. Spread 3 to 4 tablespoons pesto over each steak. Cover each with 1 tablespoon breadcrumbs. Bake until fish is opaque in center, about 10 minutes.

Preheat broiler. Broil fish until breadcrumbs on top begin to brown, about 2 minutes. Transfer fish to plates. Serve, passing remaining pesto separately, if desired.

4 SERVINGS

♦ ♦ ♦

SICILIAN SUPPER FOR FOUR

COUNTRY-STYLE BEAN AND
VEGETABLE SOUP
(PAGE 32)

CRUSTY ROLLS

BROILED SHARK WITH
PESTO TRAPANESE
(AT LEFT; PICTURED AT LEFT)

CORVO RED

STRAWBERRIES AND GRAPES WITH
MINT AND VANILLA
(PAGE 185)

♦ ♦ ♦

Tuna Burgers Niçoise

◆ ◆ ◆

1 10-ounce russet potato, pierced several times with fork

½ cup nonfat mayonnaise
4 teaspoons Dijon mustard
1 teaspoon white wine vinegar
½ teaspoon salt
¼ teaspoon pepper
½ cup finely chopped fresh basil
¼ cup diced pitted brine-cured black olives (such as Kalamata)
4 teaspoons chopped drained capers
4 teaspoons minced shallots
1 pound skinless boneless fresh tuna steaks, finely chopped

   Nonstick vegetable oil spray

4 3-inch-long pieces French bread
4 tomato slices
4 butter lettuce leaves

Cook potato in microwave until tender, about 5 minutes per side. Peel potato; mash enough to measure ¼ cup (packed).

Place ¼ cup mashed potato in bowl. Mix in ¼ cup mayonnaise, mustard, vinegar, salt and pepper, then ¼ cup basil, olives, capers and shallots. Add tuna and combine gently. Shape tuna mixture into four 1-inch-thick patties. Mix remaining ¼ cup mayonnaise and ¼ cup basil in small bowl to blend.

Prepare barbecue (medium-high heat). Spray both sides of tuna burgers with nonstick vegetable oil spray and grill until just opaque in center, about 4 minutes per side.

Cut bread pieces lengthwise into thirds; discard centers. Spread basil mayonnaise on bottom halves. Top with tuna burgers, tomatoes, lettuce and bread tops and serve.

4 SERVINGS

Low-Fat Marinated Sea Bass with Three-Citrus Sauce

♦ ♦ ♦

⅔   cup orange juice

¼   cup fresh lime juice

¼   cup fresh lemon juice

1½ teaspoons grated orange peel

¾   teaspoon grated lime peel

¾   teaspoon grated lemon peel

¼   cup minced shallots

1   tablespoon honey

1   jalapeño chili, minced

4   6-ounce sea bass fillets (each about 1 inch thick)

2   teaspoons arrowroot

Combine juices and peels in 13 x 9 x 2-inch glass baking dish. Whisk in shallots, honey and chili. Add fish; turn to coat. Cover and refrigerate 2 hours, turning fish occasionally.

Remove fish from marinade; reserve marinade. Pat fish dry with paper towels. Sprinkle fish with salt and pepper. Spray medium non-stick skillet with vegetable oil spray. Heat skillet over medium-high heat. Add fish; cook until just opaque in center, about 4 minutes per side. Using spatula, transfer fish to plates. Place arrowroot in small saucepan. Gradually whisk in marinade. Boil over medium heat until sauce thickens slightly, whisking, 2 minutes. Spoon over fish.

4 SERVINGS

♦ ♦ ♦

LIGHT DINNER FOR FOUR

LOW-FAT MARINATED SEA BASS
WITH THREE-CITRUS SAUCE
(AT LEFT; PICTURED AT LEFT)

MIXED VEGETABLE SAUTÉ
WITH GINGER
(PAGE 142; PICTURED AT LEFT)

STEAMED RICE

SAUVIGNON BLANC

ANGEL FOOD CAKE WITH
FRESH BERRIES

♦ ♦ ♦

Seared Ahi Tuna Salad

◆ ◆ ◆

DRESSING

½   cup olive oil

¼   cup fresh lime juice

¼   cup orange juice

2   tablespoons soy sauce

2   tablespoons oriental sesame oil

2   tablespoons minced fresh chives

1   tablespoon minced fresh ginger

WONTONS

    Vegetable oil (for deep-frying)

8   wonton wrappers, cut into thin strips

12   large cherry tomatoes, cut in half

2   medium carrots, peeled, cut on diagonal into thin slices

16   sugar snap peas

6   tablespoons sesame seeds

4   5-ounce fresh tuna steaks (each about ¾ to 1 inch thick)

8   ounces mixed baby lettuces

FOR DRESSING: Whisk first 7 ingredients in small bowl to blend. Season dressing with salt and pepper.

FOR WONTONS: Pour oil into heavy medium saucepan to depth of 1 inch. Heat oil to 375°F. Working in batches, fry wonton strips until golden and crisp, about 1 minute. Using tongs, transfer wonton strips to paper towels; drain well. Sprinkle with salt and pepper. *(Dressing and wonton strips can be prepared 2 hours ahead. Let stand at room temperature.)*

Place tomatoes in small bowl. Add 2 tablespoons dressing and toss to coat. Cook carrots and peas in medium pot of boiling salted water until crisp-tender, about 30 seconds. Drain, rinse with cold water and pat dry. Place carrots and peas in medium bowl; toss with 2 tablespoons dressing.

◆ ◆ ◆

ASIAN-STYLE LUNCH FOR FOUR

SEARED AHI TUNA SALAD
(AT RIGHT; PICTURED OPPOSITE)

SESAME SEED ROLLS

SPARKLING WATER OR ICED TEA

FRESH FRUIT COCKTAIL
WITH SORBET
(PAGE 185)

◆ ◆ ◆

The tuna can be quickly seared, leaving the center of the fish rare. It is also delicious when cooked until opaque in the center, as is done here.

Stir sesame seeds in heavy large skillet over high heat until seeds are pale golden, about 2 minutes. Transfer to large plate. Sprinkle fish with salt and pepper. Dip fish into seeds, coating on all sides and pressing fish so that seeds adhere. Return same skillet to high heat. Brush skillet with some of deep-frying oil. Add fish to skillet; sear until fish is just opaque in center and coating is deep brown on outside, about 3 minutes per side. Transfer fish to work surface.

Mound lettuces on 4 plates. Thinly slice fish; arrange fish, slices overlapping, on lettuces. Surround with tomatoes, carrots and peas, dividing equally. Drizzle salads with some dressing. Garnish with wonton strips. Serve, passing any remaining dressing separately.

4 SERVINGS

Lobster and Confetti Vegetable Salad

◆ ◆ ◆

1	tablespoon Dijon mustard
3	tablespoons seasoned rice vinegar*
2½	tablespoons fresh orange juice
1½	tablespoons olive oil
1½	tablespoons chopped fresh tarragon or 1½ teaspoons dried
1	large shallot, minced
1	teaspoon (packed) grated orange peel
1	large yellow bell pepper
1	large red bell pepper
2	8- to 10-ounce uncooked lobster tails (thawed, if frozen)
12	ounces small green beans, trimmed
1	large white-skinned potato, cut into ½-inch pieces
1	large ear fresh corn, kernels cut from cob
10	cups mixed baby greens (about 5 ounces)

Place mustard in small bowl. Whisk in 2 tablespoons vinegar and orange juice. Gradually whisk in oil. Mix in tarragon, shallot and orange peel. Season dressing to taste with salt and pepper.

Char bell peppers over gas flame or in broiler until blackened on all sides. Enclose in paper bag and let stand 10 minutes. Peel and seed peppers; cut into ½-inch pieces. Place in large bowl.

Bring large pot of salted water to boil. Add lobster tails; cook 10 minutes. Transfer to bowl of ice water; cool. Add green beans to same pot of boiling water; cook until crisp-tender, about 5 minutes. Using slotted spoon, transfer beans to another bowl of ice water; cool. Add potato to same pot of boiling water and cook 2 minutes. Add corn kernels; cook until potato and corn are just tender, about 2 minutes longer. Drain; add to bowl with peppers. Drain green beans; pat dry with paper towels. Add beans to potato mixture.

Drain lobster; remove meat from shells. Cut meat into rounds. *(Dressing, lobster and salad can be made 4 hours ahead. Cover separately; chill.)* Mix lobster with 1½ tablespoons dressing. Mix remaining dressing into salad. Season with salt and pepper.

Toss greens with remaining 1 tablespoon vinegar. Place on large platter. Mound salad on greens. Arrange lobster over greens and serve.

*Available at Asian markets and in some supermarkets.

4 SERVINGS

◆ ◆ ◆

DINNER ON THE PATIO FOR FOUR

CHILLED ZUCCHINI-CUMIN SOUP
(PAGE 36)

LOBSTER AND CONFETTI
VEGETABLE SALAD
(AT RIGHT; PICTURED OPPOSITE)

LAVASH

WHITE WINE SPRITZERS

PLUM GRANITA WITH
MIXED FRUIT
(PAGE 206)

ICED ESPRESSO

◆ ◆ ◆

To prepare an artichoke for cooking, first cut off the stem. Then remove the dark green outer leaves by bending the leaves backward until they snap off near the bottom.

Use a small sharp knife to cut off the dark green parts of the base and the leaf bottoms until the base is smooth and pale green.

Carefully cut out the hairy choke and spiky purple-tipped leaves from each artichoke quarter.

Artichoke Stew with Mussels, Potatoes and Saffron

◆ ◆ ◆

ARTICHOKES

2	large lemons, halved
5	medium artichokes
10	cups canned low-salt chicken broth
2	tablespoons extra-virgin olive oil
1	bay leaf

STEW

12	small red-skinned potatoes
1	tablespoon salt
1	bay leaf
1¼	teaspoons mustard seeds
½	teaspoon celery seeds
¼	teaspoon (packed) stem saffron
18	mussels, scrubbed, debearded
¾	cup chopped shallots
5	tablespoons unsalted butter
2	green onions, finely chopped
1	bunch chives, chopped

FOR ARTICHOKES: Squeeze juice from 2 lemon halves into large bowl; add lemon halves. Fill bowl with water. Cut stem off 1 artichoke. Starting at base, bend leaves back and snap off where they break naturally; continue until all tough outer leaves have been removed, leaving cone of tender pale green leaves. Using small sharp knife, trim outside edge of base until smooth and no dark green areas remain. Rub trimmed edge with 1 of remaining lemon halves. Cut artichoke lengthwise into quarters. Rub cut sides of quarters with lemon. Using small knife, cut out choke and small purple-tipped leaves from 1 quarter. Rub cut areas with lemon. Trim top leaves, leaving artichoke quarter about 2 inches long. Cut quarter into 2 wedges. Place in lemon water. Repeat with remaining artichokes.

Bring broth, olive oil and bay leaf to boil in heavy large pot (do not use aluminum or cast iron). Drain artichokes; add to pot. Return to boil. Reduce heat to medium-low; simmer until artichokes are tender, about 20 minutes. Using slotted spoon, transfer artichokes to medium bowl. Reserve 1 cup cooking liquid in small bowl.

FOR STEW: Place potatoes, salt, bay leaf, ½ teaspoon mustard seeds and celery seeds in large saucepan. Pour in enough cold water to cover potatoes generously. Boil until potatoes are tender, about 20 minutes. Drain. Cool 15 minutes; peel.

Stir saffron in heavy large pot over medium-low heat until fragrant, about 2 minutes. Add reserved 1 cup cooking liquid; bring to simmer. Add artichokes, potatoes, mussels, shallots, butter and ¾ teaspoon mustard seeds. Bring to boil. Cover pot; cook until mussels open and potatoes are golden, about 8 minutes. (Discard any unopened mussels.) Mix in onions. Season with salt and pepper.

Divide stew among 6 shallow soup bowls. Sprinkle with chives.

2 SERVINGS

Trim the tougher leaf tops from each quarter so all that remains is the choicest, most tender portion.

Shrimp with Zucchini and Tomatoes

◆ ◆ ◆

2   tablespoons plus 6 teaspoons extra-virgin olive oil
1¼ pounds baby zucchini (about 36), cut into ½-inch-thick rounds
8   ripe plum tomatoes, peeled, seeded, chopped
1½ teaspoons minced fresh rosemary

36 uncooked large shrimp, peeled, deveined

Heat 2 tablespoons oil in large skillet over medium-low heat. Add zucchini; sauté until almost tender, 3 minutes. Stir in tomatoes and rosemary. Sauté until zucchini are tender, 2 minutes.

Meanwhile, cook shrimp in large pot of boiling salted water until opaque in center, about 4 minutes. Drain shrimp. Spoon zucchini mixture onto plates. Top with shrimp. Drizzle 1 teaspoon oil over each.

6 SERVINGS

Cornmeal-crusted Oysters

◆ ◆ ◆

⅔   cup nonfat mayonnnaise
3   tablespoons finely chopped sweet pickles
2   teaspoons cider vinegar
1   garlic clove, pressed
24 fresh oysters, shucked, or about four 8-ounce jars medium oysters
1   tablespoon vegetable oil

1½ cups yellow cornmeal
¾   teaspoon salt
¾   teaspoon cayenne pepper
¼   teaspoon ground black pepper
1   cup low-fat buttermilk

Mix mayonnaise, pickles, vinegar and garlic in small bowl.
Preheat oven to 450°F. Drain oysters on paper towels. Brush large nonstick baking sheet with oil. Heat in oven 10 minutes.

Meanwhile, mix cornmeal, salt, cayenne and pepper in pie dish. Pour buttermilk into bowl. Lightly coat oysters with cornmeal. Dip into buttermilk, then coat again with cornmeal.

Place oysters on hot baking sheet, spacing apart. Bake until golden brown on bottoms, about 8 minutes. Serve with mayonnaise.

4 SERVINGS

◆ ◆ ◆

DINNER WITH CO-WORKERS FOR SIX

MIXED GREEN SALAD

SHRIMP WITH ZUCCHINI AND TOMATOES
(AT LEFT; PICTURED OPPOSITE)

PENNE WITH ASPARAGUS AND BASIL
(PAGE 125; PICTURED OPPOSITE)

CRUSTY BREAD

PINOT GRIGIO

VANILLA FROZEN YOGURT WITH MIXED BERRIES

◆ ◆ ◆

Asian Shrimp and Noodle Salad

◆ ◆ ◆

7   tablespoons bottled oil and vinegar dressing
5   to 6 teaspoons fish sauce (nam pla)* or soy sauce
4   tablespoons chopped fresh basil
1   tablespoon minced peeled fresh ginger
8   ounces cooked peeled shrimp

6   ounces thin dried Asian noodles (somen) or vermicelli
¼   unpeeled cucumber, seeded, cut into matchstick-size strips

Whisk bottled dressing, 5 teaspoons fish sauce, 3 tablespoons chopped basil and ginger in large bowl to blend. Mix shrimp into dressing and let marinate 10 minutes.

Cook noodles in medium pot of boiling salted water until just tender but still firm to bite. Drain; rinse under cold water to cool quickly. Drain again. Add noodles and cucumber to shrimp. Toss to coat. Season salad to taste with salt and pepper; add remaining 1 teaspoon fish sauce, if desired. Divide salad between 2 plates. Sprinkle with remaining 1 tablespoon basil and serve.

*Nam pla *is available at Asian markets and in the Asian foods section of some supermarkets.*

2 SERVINGS

◆ ◆ ◆

Somen are very thin Japanese noodles made from flour and water, with no egg. They are used in broths as well as in cold dishes, such as the shrimp and noodle salad here.

◆ ◆ ◆

Seared Scallops with Tarragon Cream

◆ ◆ ◆

1¼   pounds (about 20) large sea scallops
1   teaspoon vegetable oil

1½   teaspoons butter
1   tablespoon all purpose flour
1   cup low-fat (1%) milk
2   tablespoons chopped fresh tarragon

Pat scallops dry. Sprinkle with salt and pepper. Heat oil in heavy large skillet over high heat. Add scallops; cook until brown on bottom, about 3 minutes. Turn scallops over; cook until opaque in center, about 1 minute longer. Transfer scallops to plate. Tent with foil.

Reduce heat to medium. Melt butter in same skillet. Add flour; stir 1 minute. Gradually whisk in milk. Simmer until thick and smooth, stirring often, about 3 minutes. Stir in tarragon and any juices from scallops on plate. Season with salt and pepper. Spoon onto plates. Arrange scallops, brown side up, atop sauce.

4 SERVINGS

◆ ◆ ◆

FAMILY SEAFOOD DINNER FOR FOUR

SEARED SCALLOPS WITH
TARRAGON CREAM
(AT LEFT; PICTURED AT LEFT)

SPRING PEAS WITH
LETTUCE AND MINT
(PAGE 144; PICTURED AT LEFT)

STEAMED RED POTATOES

ICED TEA

NEW-STYLE OLD-FASHIONED
CHOCOLATE PUDDING
(PAGE 197)

◆ ◆ ◆

Eggplant with Roasted Pepper, Olive and Feta Salad

◆ ◆ ◆

2	large red bell peppers
½	cup drained canned garbanzo beans (chickpeas)
½	cup brine-cured black olives (such as Kalamata), pitted, halved
4	ounces feta cheese, crumbled
2	tablespoons chopped fresh oregano
¼	cup balsamic vinegar
2	tablespoons minced garlic
4	teaspoons soy sauce
½	cup olive oil
1	1½-pound eggplant
	Fresh oregano sprigs
4	6-inch-diameter pita breads, cut into wedges, lightly toasted

Char bell peppers over gas flame or in broiler until blackened on all sides. Enclose in bag; let stand 10 minutes. Peel and seed peppers. Cut into ½-inch pieces. Transfer peppers to large bowl. Add beans, olives, cheese and chopped oregano and toss to combine. Season salad to taste with salt and pepper.

Whisk vinegar, garlic and soy sauce in small bowl. Gradually whisk in oil. Season dressing with salt and pepper.

Preheat broiler. Cut six ½-inch-thick lengthwise slices from center of eggplant. Arrange eggplant on baking sheet. Brush both sides of eggplant with some of dressing. Sprinkle with salt and pepper. Broil until golden, about 2 minutes per side.

Place 1 eggplant slice on each plate. Spoon salad over. Drizzle with dressing. Garnish with oregano. Serve with pita.

6 SERVINGS

Spiced Basmati Rice with Lentils and Caramelized Onions

◆ ◆ ◆

1   tablespoon butter
4   cups sliced onions

½   cup dried lentils

2½   cups water
3   whole cardamom pods
2   whole allspice
1   bay leaf
1   teaspoon salt
1   cup basmati rice* or long-grain white rice

Melt butter in 10-inch-diameter ovenproof nonstick skillet over medium-low heat. Add onions and stir 1 minute. Cover and cook until onions are tender, stirring occasionally, about 15 minutes. Uncover and sauté until onions are deep golden, about 5 minutes longer. Season to taste with salt and pepper. Remove from heat. Spread onions in even layer in same skillet; set aside.

Meanwhile, cook lentils in pot of boiling water until almost tender but still firm to bite, about 20 minutes. Drain.

Combine 2½ cups water, cardamom, allspice, bay leaf and salt in heavy medium saucepan; bring to boil. Add rice and lentils and bring to boil. Reduce heat to low. Cover and simmer until rice is tender and water is absorbed, about 15 minutes. Discard cardamom pods, allspice and bay leaf.

Preheat oven to 400°F. Spoon rice mixture atop onions in skillet, pressing with back of spoon to compact rice; smooth top. *(Rice mixture can be prepared 2 hours ahead. Cool. Cover skillet and let stand at room temperature.)*

Cover skillet tightly with double layer of foil. Bake rice mixture until heated through, about 35 minutes. Remove foil; let stand 5 minutes. Place plate over skillet; invert skillet, releasing rice and onions onto plate and scraping any onions remaining in skillet onto rice. Spoon rice and onions onto plates and serve.

Available at Indian markets and many supermarkets.

4 SERVINGS

INDIAN DINNER FOR FOUR

Pumpkin-Corn Cakes with Tomatillo Salsa

◆ ◆ ◆

2½ tablespoons (or more) vegetable oil
½   cup chopped onion
½   cup frozen corn kernels, thawed
⅓   cup finely chopped red bell pepper
1   tablespoon minced garlic
1   teaspoon chili powder
½   teaspoon ground cumin

⅓   cup canned solid pack pumpkin
¼   cup cottage cheese
1   large egg
1   slice (about 1 ounce) firm-textured white bread,
     crust removed, cubed
1   cup grated Monterey Jack cheese with jalapeños
½   cup dry breadcrumbs
     All purpose flour

     Purchased tomatillo salsa

Heat 1½ tablespoons oil in medium skillet over medium heat. Add onion; sauté until tender, about 7 minutes. Add next 5 ingredients; sauté until vegetables are heated through, 3 minutes. Cool.

Puree pumpkin, cottage cheese, egg and bread in processor. Transfer to large bowl. Mix in vegetables, Jack cheese and breadcrumbs. Season with salt and pepper. With floured hands, form mixture by ½ cupfuls into six 3-inch-diameter patties.

Heat 1 tablespoon oil in large skillet over medium-low heat. Working in batches, add patties to skillet; cook until golden, adding more oil as necessary, about 5 minutes per side. Serve with salsa.

MAKES 6

THE EVOLUTION OF SALSA

In Mexico, no meal is complete without a bowl of spicy fresh *salsa de molcajete*, or "table sauce," a chunky mix of fresh tomatoes, herbs and chilies used to add flavor and color to rice, tacos, meat and fish. Along with the exploding popularity of Mexican food in this country, salsa has become a staple. These days, it's as popular with tortilla chips as sour cream dip is with potato chips.

In recent years, American cooks have taken the salsa idea and made it their own, substituting fruits or other ingredients for the tomato. Pineapple, melon, corn and zucchini are often used, with chilies thrown in for that unique balance of flavors typical of traditional Mexican salsas. In the pumpkin-corn cakes at left, salsa made with tomatillos (a green tomato-like vegetable with a paper-thin husk) plays a starring role. But any prepared salsa will make for equally delicious results.

◆ ◆ ◆

Risotto with Radicchio

◆ ◆ ◆

5 cups (about) vegetable broth

3 tablespoons extra-virgin olive oil
1 cup finely chopped onion
1½ cups arborio rice* (about 10 ounces)
½ cup dry white wine

2 cups finely chopped radicchio
⅓ cup freshly grated Parmesan cheese
¼ cup half and half
3 tablespoons chopped fresh Italian parsley
1 teaspoon chopped fresh thyme

Additional freshly grated Parmesan cheese

Bring 5 cups broth to simmer in heavy medium saucepan over medium-high heat. Reduce heat to low; keep broth hot.

Heat oil in heavy large saucepan over medium heat. Add onion; sauté until soft but not brown, about 5 minutes. Add rice; stir 2 minutes. Add wine; reduce heat to medium-low. Simmer until wine is absorbed, stirring constantly, about 1 minute. Add 1 cup hot broth; simmer until broth is absorbed, stirring often, about 3 minutes. Continue adding broth ½ cup at a time until rice is tender but still slightly firm in center and mixture is creamy, simmering until broth is absorbed before each addition and stirring often, about 20 minutes.

Mix 1½ cups radicchio into risotto; simmer 3 minutes, stirring often. Remove risotto from heat. Mix in ⅓ cup Parmesan cheese, half and half, parsley and thyme. Season to taste with salt and pepper.

Transfer risotto to shallow serving bowl. Sprinkle with ½ cup radicchio. Serve, passing additional Parmesan.

*Arborio is an Italian short-grain rice that is available at Italian markets and some supermarkets.

4 SERVINGS

Soften the chopped onion in olive oil. Then add the rice, and stir until it's well coated with the oil.

Add wine to the rice, and simmer until wine is absorbed. Next, stir in a cup of broth, and simmer until it, too, is absorbed. At this point, the rice is still hard and in separate grains.

Stir in a small amount of broth every few minutes so that the rice softens and releases its starch gradually, creating a creamy texture.

GOING GREEK

In addition to olive oil, a staple in Greek cooking, the well-stocked Greek kitchen will contain the following, each lending its own special flavor to any number of dishes.

◆ Kalamata Olives: Native to the Kalamata region of Greece, these purple-black, almond-shaped olives are sturdy and snappy in flavor. Greek cooks use them in everything from salads to stews to bread.

◆ Feta Cheese: With a flavor ranging from mellow and creamy to sharp and assertive (depending on the milk used to make it), this unique cheese may be sliced, cubed or crumbled and added to salads, pastas and more.

◆ Mint: Liberally used, mint finds its way into stews and vegetable dishes and is often paired with cheese.

◆ Oregano: The aromatic leaves are often chopped and added to salads and meat dishes (it has a natural affinity for lamb).

◆ Honey: Greek bees feed off herbal flowers such as thyme. The resulting honey is strong in flavor and inextricably linked to the national sweet, baklava.

◆ Phyllo: Thin as tissue paper, phyllo is the pastry dough of Greece.

◆ ◆ ◆

Greek Salad Submarine Sandwich

◆ ◆ ◆

½ cup olive oil
6 tablespoons fresh lemon juice
¼ cup chopped fresh basil
2 tablespoons chopped fresh mint
2 tablespoons chopped fresh oregano or 2 teaspoons dried

1 1-pound loaf French bread, sliced horizontally in half
8 ounces feta cheese, crumbled (about 2 cups)
12 brine-cured black olives (such as Kalamata), pitted, halved
3 large plum tomatoes, thinly sliced
1 green bell pepper, thinly sliced
½ red onion, thinly sliced
½ cucumber, peeled, thinly sliced
3 peperoncini peppers from jar, drained, coarsely chopped

Combine first 5 ingredients in small bowl; whisk to blend. Season dressing to taste with salt and pepper.

Spoon ¾ cup dressing evenly over cut side of bottom half of bread. Sprinkle cheese over bread. Top with even layers of olives, tomatoes, bell pepper, onion, cucumber and peperoncini. Pull or cut away enough bread from top half to leave ½-inch-thick shell. Spoon remaining dressing over peperoncini. Place top of bread over filling. Press to compact. Cut sandwich into 4 to 6 even sections.

4 TO 6 SERVINGS

Tarragon, Chive and Goat Cheese Omelet

◆ ◆ ◆

5   large eggs
2   tablespoons chopped fresh tarragon
1   tablespoon chopped fresh chives
1   tablespoon chopped fresh parsley
½   teaspoon salt
¼   teaspoon pepper
2   tablespoons (¼ stick) butter
1¼   cups crumbled soft fresh goat cheese (such as Montrachet; about 4 ounces)

Whisk first 6 ingredients in medium bowl to blend. Melt 1 tablespoon butter in 9- to 10-inch-diameter nonstick skillet over medium heat. Add half of egg mixture to skillet; cook until very softly set, tilting skillet, running rubber spatula around edges and allowing uncooked egg portion to flow underneath, about 2 minutes. Sprinkle half of goat cheese over. Cover; cook until omelet is set, about 2 minutes. Tilt skillet and slide out omelet onto plate, folding omelet in half. Cover to keep warm. Repeat for second omelet with remaining butter, egg mixture and goat cheese. Serve immediately.

2 SERVINGS

Italian Spoon Biscuits with Tomato Sauce and Cheese

◆ ◆ ◆

3   10- to 11-ounce cans refrigerated buttermilk biscuits
2   cups prepared tomato pasta sauce
1   cup sliced green onions
1   green bell pepper, chopped
2   cups (packed) grated mozzarella cheese (about 8 ounces)

Preheat oven to 350°F. Butter 13 x 9 x 2-inch glass baking dish. Cut each biscuit into 8 pieces; place in prepared dish. Add sauce, green onions and bell pepper and stir to blend well.

Bake until top is set and almost firm to touch, about 35 minutes. Sprinkle cheese over evenly. Bake until cheese melts, about 5 minutes longer. Let stand 10 minutes. Cut into squares and serve.

8 SERVINGS

◆ ◆ ◆

This unusual dish—which combines biscuits, tomato sauce and mozzarella cheese—is a cross between a meatless lasagna and a pizza bread. It makes a terrific quick supper.

◆ ◆ ◆

Porcini Mushroom Shepherd's Pies

◆ ◆ ◆

2	cups water
1	ounce dried porcini mushrooms
1½	cups milk
2	pounds russet potatoes, peeled, cut into 1-inch pieces
8	tablespoons (1 stick) butter
2½	cups 1-inch pieces green beans (about 8 ounces)
3	carrots, cut into ¼-inch-thick slices
2	cups frozen corn kernels
1½	cups chopped onions
1	pound mushrooms, sliced
3	tablespoons all purpose flour
4	teaspoons soy sauce
1½	teaspoons dried thyme

Bring water and porcini to boil in small saucepan. Reduce heat to medium-low; simmer until liquid is reduced to ¾ cup, about 25 minutes. Using slotted spoon, transfer porcini to cutting board. Coarsely chop porcini. Transfer to bowl and reserve. Strain liquid into 2-cup measuring cup, leaving any sandy residue behind. Add ¾ cup milk to porcini liquid; reserve.

Cook potatoes in large pot of boiling salted water until very tender, about 20 minutes. Drain. Transfer potatoes to large bowl. Add remaining ¾ cup milk and 5 tablespoons butter. Using electric mixer, beat until smooth. Season with salt and pepper.

Cook green beans and carrots in large pot of boiling salted water 3 minutes. Add corn and boil until all vegetables are tender, about 3 minutes longer. Drain well.

Preheat oven to 400°F. Butter eight 1¼-cup custard cups. Melt 3 tablespoons butter in large skillet over medium heat. Add onions; sauté until golden, about 8 minutes. Stir in sliced mushrooms

◆ ◆ ◆

Porcini, plenty of vegetables, some thyme and soy sauce give this meatless dish its rich flavor. The dried mushrooms are available at Italian markets, specialty foods stores and many supermarkets.

◆ ◆ ◆

and porcini. Cover and cook 5 minutes. Uncover; cook until almost all liquid is absorbed, about 6 minutes. Add flour; stir 2 minutes. Stir in soy sauce, thyme and porcini liquid. Bring to boil, stirring. Reduce heat; simmer to thicken sauce, about 2 minutes. Stir in vegetables. Divide among custard cups. Spoon potatoes over; smooth tops. Bake until golden, about 15 minutes.

MAKES 8

Spanish-Style Tortilla

◆ ◆ ◆

10 ounces red-skinned potatoes, cut into ⅓-inch pieces

8 large eggs
4 teaspoons minced fresh parsley
2 teaspoons minced fresh oregano
1 teaspoon salt
½ teaspoon dried crushed red pepper
⅛ teaspoon pepper
1 tablespoon olive oil
1 medium onion, chopped

Position rack in center of oven and preheat to 350°F. Cook potatoes in large saucepan of boiling salted water until tender, about 6 minutes. Drain well and cool.

Whisk eggs and next 5 ingredients in large bowl until blended. Mix in potatoes. Heat oil in large ovenproof nonstick skillet over high heat. Add onion; sauté until golden, about 5 minutes. Reduce heat to medium. Add egg mixture; cook 3 minutes, occasionally stirring egg from sides of skillet. Place skillet in oven; bake eggs until set in center and no longer wet on top, about 20 minutes.

Remove tortilla from oven. Immediately place skillet on cold wet kitchen towel to prevent further cooking. Let stand 2 minutes. Run spatula around edge of skillet and under tortilla. Lift skillet and tilt, sliding tortilla onto platter. Serve tortilla either warm or at room temperature. Cut into wedges.

4 SERVINGS

◆ ◆ ◆

This classic Spanish egg-and-potato dish is similar to a frittata. It can be served either warm or at room temperature, making it a practical recipe for casual entertaining.

◆ ◆ ◆

◆

◆

MEATLESS SUPPER FOR EIGHT

POLENTA LASAGNA WITH
ESCAROLE AND THREE CHEESES
(AT RIGHT; PICTURED OPPOSITE)

MIXED GREEN SALAD

GARLIC BREAD

CHIANTI

CHOCOLATE AND ALMOND SPUMONI
(PAGE 208)

◆ ◆ ◆

Polenta Lasagna with Escarole and Three Cheeses

◆ ◆ ◆

3¾ cups water
1½ cups yellow cornmeal
1   teaspoon salt

3   tablespoons olive oil
1   medium head escarole, chopped
1   cup chopped onion
1   28-ounce can crushed tomatoes with added puree
½   cup chopped fresh basil
2   tablespoons tomato paste
4   teaspoons minced garlic

6   ounces Neufchâtel cheese (reduced-fat cream cheese),
     room temperature
1   large egg
1   cup grated Parmesan cheese

2   cups grated Monterey Jack cheese

Butter 9 x 5 x 2½-inch loaf pan. Bring water, cornmeal and salt to boil in heavy large saucepan, whisking constantly. Reduce heat to medium-low; whisk until mixture is very thick, about 5 minutes. Transfer to prepared pan; smooth top. Cover and refrigerate until firm, at least 3 hours or overnight.

Heat oil in large pot over medium heat. Add escarole; sauté until wilted, about 3 minutes. Add onion; sauté until tender, about 8 minutes. Mix in crushed tomatoes, basil, tomato paste and garlic. Simmer 10 minutes to blend flavors. Season sauce with salt and pepper.

Using electric mixer, beat Neufchâtel cheese in large bowl until fluffy. Beat in egg, then Parmesan cheese.

Preheat oven to 400°F. Oil 8 x 8 x 2-inch glass baking dish. Turn polenta out onto work surface. Using serrated knife, cut into 20 slices. Spoon ⅓ of sauce over bottom of prepared dish. Arrange 10 polenta slices atop sauce, overlapping slightly. Spoon ⅓ of sauce over. Drop cheese mixture by small spoonfuls over. Arrange 10 polenta slices atop. Spoon remaining sauce over. Sprinkle Monterey Jack cheese over. *(Can be made 1 day ahead; chill.)* Place dish on baking sheet. Bake until cheese melts and sauce bubbles around edges, about 35 minutes. Cool 10 minutes and serve.

8 SERVINGS

Spinach Gnocchi with Fontina Cheese

♦ ♦ ♦

1	pound russet potatoes
2	10-ounce packages ready-to-use spinach leaves, stemmed
1	small egg, beaten to blend
¼	teaspoon ground nutmeg
1½	cups (about) all purpose flour
¼	cup (½ stick) butter, melted
5	ounces Fontina cheese, thinly sliced

Steam potatoes until tender, about 35 minutes. Cool potatoes slightly; peel. Mash potatoes in large bowl until smooth. Set aside.

Meanwhile, bring 2 inches of salted water to boil in large pot. Add spinach to pot and cook until wilted, stirring occasionally, about 2 minutes. Drain spinach, reserving ¼ cup cooking liquid. Squeeze liquid from spinach. Puree spinach in processor, adding reserved cooking liquid by tablespoonfuls if necessary to moisten, and scraping down sides of processor occasionally.

Transfer spinach mixture to bowl with potatoes. Mix in egg, ground nutmeg and enough flour until soft and slightly sticky dough forms. Season dough to taste with salt.

Dust baking sheet with flour. Working in batches and using floured hands, roll ¼ cup dough on lightly floured work surface to form 12-inch rope. Cut rope into 1-inch pieces. Roll each piece between palms to form oval ball. Lightly flour the wires of a whisk. Using thumb, gently roll each ball down length of wires, making ribbed impressions in gnocchi. Transfer gnocchi to prepared baking sheet. Repeat rolling, cutting and shaping of remaining dough.

Preheat oven to 400°F. Butter 13 x 9-inch baking dish. Working in batches, add gnocchi to large pot of boiling salted water and cook until gnocchi rise to surface of water, about 4 minutes. Using slotted spoon, remove gnocchi from water, draining off excess, and transfer to prepared baking dish. Pour ¼ cup melted butter over gnocchi; toss thoroughly to coat. Top with Fontina cheese slices. *(Gnocchi can be made 1 day ahead. Cover and chill.)* Bake until gnocchi are heated through and cheese bubbles, about 10 minutes.

4 SERVINGS

Spinach adds color and flavor to these light potato-and-flour dumplings, called *gnocchi* in Italian cooking. The topping, which consists of melted butter and Fontina cheese, gives this pasta dish its rich taste.

♦ ♦ ♦

Orecchiette with Mushrooms, Arugula, Tomatoes and Brie

◆ ◆ ◆

2   cups orecchiette or small pasta shells (about ½ pound)

2   tablespoons olive oil (preferably extra-virgin)
6   ounces portobello mushrooms, thinly sliced
2   large garlic cloves, minced
¾   pound plum tomatoes, chopped
½   cup dry white wine

2   bunches arugula, stems trimmed
¼   pound Brie, rind trimmed, cheese cut into ½-inch pieces

Cook orecchiette in pot of boiling salted water until just tender but still firm to bite. Drain, reserving ½ cup cooking liquid.

Meanwhile, heat oil in heavy large skillet over medium-high heat. Add mushrooms and garlic and sauté until mushrooms soften, about 5 minutes. Add tomatoes and stir until beginning to soften, about 2 minutes. Add wine and bring sauce to boil. Reduce heat to medium-low; simmer until tomatoes release their juices, 5 minutes.

Add arugula, cheese and orecchiette to sauce. Toss until arugula wilts, cheese begins to melt and orecchiette is heated through, adding reserved cooking liquid by tablespoonfuls if mixture is dry. Season to taste with salt and pepper.

2 SERVINGS

◆ ◆ ◆

Orecchiette means "little ears" in Italian, and the indented pasta disks do indeed resemble ears. Here, the pasta is combined with portobello mushrooms, tomatoes, Brie and arugula—with delicious results.

◆ ◆ ◆

HEALTH ON THE HALF SHELL

There is good news on the health front: Shellfish, with the exception of shrimp and crayfish, are not as high in cholesterol as previously reported, and in fact compare favorably to skinless chicken breast. Ounce per ounce, mollusks such as clams, mussels, oysters and scallops actually have fewer calories than skinless boneless chicken breast meat.

Also encouraging is that shellfish in general are a terrific source of protein and an equally good source of minerals like copper, iron and zinc. Zinc is essential to the proper functioning of our immune systems, but it can be hard to come by, especially for people who have cut back on red meat. Oysters in particular are an excellent source of the mineral.

Add to all these attributes wonderful flavor and an ability to adapt to different preparations (at right, clams steamed in a fennel-infused broth make a delicious addition to linguine) and you have every reason to return shellfish to the shopping list.

◆ ◆ ◆

Linguine and Clams with Tomato-Fennel Salsa

◆ ◆ ◆

2   cups chopped seeded tomatoes (about 4 large)
½   cup chopped fresh fennel bulb
¼   cup chopped red onion
3   tablespoons (packed) chopped fresh basil
1   tablespoon olive oil (preferably extra-virgin)
½   teaspoon (packed) grated orange peel

2   cups dry white wine
1   teaspoon fennel seeds
1   teaspoon salt
1   large garlic clove, crushed
30   littleneck clams, scrubbed

12   ounces linguine

Combine tomatoes, chopped fennel, red onion, basil, olive oil and orange peel in medium bowl. Season salsa with salt and pepper.

Bring wine, fennel seeds, salt and garlic to boil in very large pot. Reduce heat, cover tightly and simmer 10 minutes to blend flavors. Add clams. Increase heat to high, cover and cook until clams open, about 7 minutes (discard any clams that do not open). Using slotted spoon, transfer clams to bowl. Strain clam cooking liquid through fine strainer; return to same pot. Boil until clam cooking liquid is reduced to 1⅔ cups, about 7 minutes. Add tomato salsa and bring to simmer. Remove from heat.

Meanwhile, cook linguine in large pot of boiling salted water until tender but still firm to bite. Drain.

Add linguine to pot with tomato mixture. Season with salt and pepper; toss to blend. Add clams and stir over medium heat until heated through, about 3 minutes.

6 SERVINGS

Penne with Asparagus and Basil

◆ ◆ ◆

2	tablespoons extra-virgin olive oil
4	garlic cloves, minced
	Pinch of dried crushed red pepper
1	pound asparagus, stalks cut into ½-inch lengths
4	tomatoes, peeled, seeded, chopped
1	cup chicken stock or canned low-salt chicken broth
¼	cup thinly sliced fresh basil
8	ounces penne pasta
⅓	cup freshly grated Parmesan cheese
¼	cup chopped fresh Italian parsley
¼	cup finely chopped fresh basil

Heat oil in heavy large skillet over medium-high heat. Add garlic and red pepper; sauté until garlic is golden, about 2 minutes. Add asparagus, tomatoes, stock and ¼ cup sliced basil. Cook until asparagus is crisp-tender, about 8 minutes. Season sauce to taste with salt and pepper. Remove from heat.

Meanwhile, cook pasta in large pot of boiling salted water until tender but still firm to bite. Drain. Transfer to large bowl.

Pour sauce over pasta. Add cheese, parsley and ¼ cup chopped basil. Toss to coat. Season with salt and pepper.

2 TO 3 SERVINGS

◆ ◆ ◆

Here's a light pasta dish that comes together quickly. Served in smaller portions, it can also be offered as either a first course or a side dish.

◆ ◆ ◆

Authentic Italian cooking is generally very healthful, in large part because it is based on grains, fresh vegetables and fish, and judicious amounts of oil, cheese and meat. Here's a look at the building blocks of traditional Italian cooking.

- Basil: This herb adds a wonderful flavor, no fat or cholesterol and only a small number of calories.
- Garlic: Eaten daily in sufficient quantities, garlic can lower LDL (bad) cholesterol in the blood system and boost the immune system.
- Olive Oil: Compared to many other cooking oils, olive oil is low in saturated fat and high in monounsaturated fat—the kind thought to keep arteries clear.
- Parmesan Cheese: A tablespoon of grated Parmesan cheese sprinkled over a salad or pasta adds a big flavor boost, with only 28 calories and two grams of fat.
- Pasta: Not only is pasta a good source of carbohydrates, protein and fiber, it is also a low-fat food.
- Tomatoes: This member of the fruit family is rich in vitamin C and lycopene, an antioxidant that gives the tomato its deep red color.

◆ ◆ ◆

Rigatoni with Eggplant, Artichokes and Bell Pepper

◆ ◆ ◆

1	1¼-pound eggplant, unpeeled, cut into 1½-inch pieces
2	teaspoons salt
2	cups olive oil
4	large shallots, peeled, quartered
1	large red bell pepper
½	cup chopped pitted brine-cured black olives (such as Kalamata)
2	large garlic cloves, finely chopped
2	large artichokes, stems trimmed
8	ounces rigatoni or other tubular pasta

Preheat oven to 400°F. Toss eggplant pieces with 2 teaspoons salt in large bowl. Turn eggplant out onto paper towels and let drain 30 minutes. Pat eggplant pieces dry.

Heat oil in heavy medium saucepan over medium-high heat to 350°F. Working in batches, add eggplant to oil and cook until golden, turning occasionally, about 6 minutes per batch. Using slotted spoon, transfer eggplant to clean paper towels. Reserve 5 tablespoons eggplant frying oil. Toss shallots and whole bell pepper with 3 tablespoons reserved oil on large baking sheet. Roast until shallots are tender, turning occasionally, about 25 minutes. Place shallots and eggplant in large bowl. Continue roasting bell pepper until skin blackens, about 10 minutes. Wrap in plastic bag; let stand 10 minutes. Peel, core and seed pepper. Cut into thin strips lengthwise, then cut strips crosswise in half. Add bell pepper strips, olives and garlic to eggplant and shallots in bowl.

Cook artichokes in large pot of boiling salted water until tender, turning occasionally, about 40 minutes. Using tongs, transfer to bowl; cool. Remove leaves from artichokes and reserve for another use. Scoop out chokes. Cut artichoke hearts into ⅓-inch pieces; combine with other vegetables. *(Can be made 2 hours ahead. Cover and let stand at room temperature.)*

Cook pasta in large pot of boiling salted water until just tender but still firm to bite, stirring occasionally. Drain. Return pasta to pot. Add all vegetables and remaining 2 tablespoons reserved eggplant frying oil and toss over medium heat until heated through. Season with salt and pepper. Divide pasta among plates and serve.

4 SERVINGS

Spicy Singapore Noodles with Beef and Carrots

◆ ◆ ◆

16 ounces dried thin Chinese rice sticks (maifun)

1 tablespoon vegetable oil
4 teaspoons minced peeled fresh ginger
1 tablespoon minced garlic
1 cup thinly sliced peeled carrots
8 ounces flank steak, trimmed, thinly sliced crosswise, then cut crosswise again into ½-inch strips
½ cup plus 2 tablespoons low-sodium soy sauce
¾ teaspoon curry powder
¾ teaspoon ground cumin
¼ to ½ teaspoon dried crushed red pepper
1 cup sliced green onions

Place noodles in large bowl. Add enough hot water to cover. Let stand until noodles are tender and pliable, about 30 minutes. Drain. Rinse with cold water. Drain well.

Heat oil in large nonstick skillet over high heat. Add ginger and garlic; stir 10 seconds. Add carrots; stir 1 minute. Add steak; toss until no longer pink, about 30 seconds. Stir in soy sauce, curry, cumin and crushed red pepper. Add noodles to skillet; toss until coated with mixture and heated through, about 5 minutes. Transfer to bowl. Sprinkle green onions over and serve.

6 SERVINGS

Chinese rice sticks, also called *maifun*, are dried rice flour noodles available in different widths and lengths. They're opaque and brittle when dry but turn white and slippery once they're cooked. They are delicious in this spicy beef dish. Be sure to partially freeze the flank steak for about half an hour to make it easier to slice.

◆ ◆ ◆

Fettuccine with Sweet Pepper-Cayenne Sauce

♦ ♦ ♦

3	tablespoons butter
2	large red bell peppers, cut into ¼-inch-thick strips
3	garlic cloves, minced
¾	teaspoon cayenne pepper
1	cup whipping cream
¾	cup canned low-salt chicken broth
¾	cup grated Parmesan cheese
12	ounces fettuccine
1	cup frozen green peas
½	cup chopped fresh basil

Melt butter in heavy large skillet over medium heat. Add bell peppers, garlic and cayenne; stir to blend. Cover skillet; cook until peppers are tender, stirring occasionally, about 7 minutes. Uncover; add cream and broth and simmer until liquid is slightly thickened, about 5 minutes. Stir in ½ cup Parmesan. Remove from heat.

Meanwhile, cook fettuccine in large pot of boiling salted water until just tender but still firm to bite. Add peas to pot. Drain. Return fettuccine and peas to pot. Add bell pepper mixture and fresh basil; toss well. Season to taste with salt and pepper. Transfer to large bowl. Sprinkle with ¼ cup Parmesan and serve.

4 SERVINGS

Pasta Primavera with Smoky Ham

♦ ♦ ♦

6	ounces bow-tie pasta (about 2½ cups)
12	thin asparagus spears, stems trimmed, stalks thinly sliced into rounds, tips left whole
½	large red bell pepper, cut into thin strips
6	ounces smoked ham, diced
½	cup whipping cream
½	cup canned low-salt chicken broth
2½	tablespoons coarse-grained Dijon mustard

Cook pasta in large pot of boiling salted water 7 minutes. Add asparagus and cook 3 minutes. Add bell pepper. Boil until pasta and asparagus are just tender but still firm to bite and bell pepper strips are slightly softened, about 30 seconds longer. Drain well.

Meanwhile, stir ham in heavy large skillet over medium-high heat until beginning to brown, about 3 minutes. Add cream, broth and mustard; boil sauce 2 minutes, stirring up any browned bits.

Add pasta mixture to skillet. Toss until sauce coats pasta mixture, about 2 minutes. Season to taste with salt and pepper and serve.

2 SERVINGS

Creamy Linguine with Smoked Salmon and Peas

◆ ◆ ◆

3   cups whipping cream
3   cups bottled clam juice
2½   teaspoons grated lemon peel

2   pounds linguine
2   10-ounce packages frozen petite peas

1½   pounds thinly sliced smoked salmon, cut into ½-inch-wide strips
8   tablespoons chopped fresh dill

     Chopped green onions

Combine cream, clam juice and 1½ teaspoons lemon peel in heavy medium saucepan. Boil until reduced by half, about 15 minutes. Season with salt and pepper. *(Can be made 1 day ahead. Chill.)*

Cook pasta in large pot of boiling salted water until almost tender. Add peas and cook until pasta is tender but still firm to bite and peas are tender, about 2 minutes. Drain pasta and peas. Divide between 2 large serving bowls.

Bring sauce to simmer. Pour over pasta in bowls; toss gently. Add ¾ pound smoked salmon, 3 tablespoons dill and ½ teaspoon lemon peel to each bowl and toss. Season with salt and pepper.

Divide pasta among plates. Garnish with remaining 2 tablespoons dill and green onions. Serve immediately.

10 SERVINGS

ABOUT SMOKED SALMON

A good piece of smoked salmon should be pale to medium orange-pink in color and tender, with a silky texture and a balance of salty and smoky flavors. Most smoked salmon is identified by the country or region where it is produced. Here are the best types.

◆ Scottish: Many consider Scottish smoked salmon to be the prize among all the varieties. Imported from Scotland, this type is known for its excellent texture and smoky yet rather delicate flavor.

◆ Norwegian: Producing 70 percent of the world's farmed salmon, Norway has a large (and respected) salmon smoking industry. Norwegian smoked salmon is soft, with a consistently good, mild flavor.

◆ Irish: Generally drier and smokier than its Scottish and Norwegian counterparts, Irish smoked salmon also tends to be saltier and meatier.

◆ Pacific Northwest: Since Pacific salmon have less fat than North Atlantic salmon, the smoked salmon from this region is drier than the imported kinds. The flavor is still good, though. Northwestern smoked salmon is produced from five different species, including chinook, sockeye and chum.

◆ ◆ ◆

KEEPING PASTA LIGHT

The fusilli at right proves that a pasta recipe can taste great and still be very low in fat. Here are a few suggestions on how to keep all of your pasta dishes low in fat, yet still rich tasting and satisfying.

◆ Vegetables: Use a generous combination of substantial ones, like cauliflower, broccoli and wild mushrooms. It will seem as though you're getting more to eat.

◆ Canned tomatoes: Use them to make tomato-based sauces instead of those with butter and cream.

◆ Pasta shape: Bulkier shapes like fusilli, penne, rigatoni or shells hold sauces better than thin strand pastas. Plus, they look like more food on your plate.

◆ High-flavor ingredients: Small portions of roasted red bell peppers, anchovies, olives, smoked salmon, and such cheeses as Parmesan and Romano go a long way. You can get away with using just a little for a lot of flavor, without greatly increasing fat and calories.

◆ Pureed ingredients: Canned white beans, cooked carrots, olives, anchovies, canned tomatoes and roasted bell peppers can be pureed and used to help thicken sauces.

◆ ◆ ◆

Pasta with Sausage, Bell Peppers, Onions and Basil

◆ ◆ ◆

¼   cup extra-virgin olive oil
3   pounds sweet Italian sausage, crumbled
5   cups sliced onions (1¼ pounds)
2   red bell peppers, cut into strips
1½ cups dry white wine

2   pounds short pasta (such as fusilli)
1½ cups freshly grated Parmesan
2   cups thinly sliced fresh basil
    Additional freshly grated Parmesan

Divide oil between 2 heavy large skillets over medium heat. Divide sausage between skillets; cook until brown, crumbling with spoon, about 12 minutes. Using slotted spoon, transfer sausage to large bowl. Add onions to skillets, dividing equally. Sauté until golden, about 10 minutes. Add bell peppers to onions, dividing equally. Sauté until tender, about 6 minutes. Pour ¾ cup wine into each skillet and boil 5 minutes to allow wine to evaporate slightly. Add bell peppers and onions to sausage.

Cook pasta in large pot of boiling salted water until just tender but still firm to bite, stirring occasionally. Drain pasta. Return to pot. Add sausage and vegetables; toss. Mix in 1½ cups cheese. Add 1½ cups basil; toss. Season with salt and pepper. Mound in bowl. Sprinkle with ½ cup basil. Serve, passing additional cheese.

12 SERVINGS

Fusilli with Porcini Puttanesca Sauce

◆ ◆ ◆

1⅓ cups hot water
½   ounce (about ¾ cup) dried porcini mushrooms*

1   28-ounce can diced tomatoes in juice
1¼ cups finely chopped onion
1½ tablespoons minced garlic
12 Niçoise olives,** pitted, chopped
2   tablespoons tomato paste

1½   tablespoons drained capers

1½   tablespoons chopped anchovy fillets

1   teaspoon dried oregano

1   teaspoon dried basil

⅛   teaspoon dried crushed red pepper

8   ounces fusilli pasta

Combine 1⅓ cups hot water and porcini mushrooms in small bowl. Let stand until porcini are soft, about 25 minutes. Strain porcini, reserving liquid; discard sandy residue from porcini in bottom of bowl. Coarsely chop porcini.

Drain tomatoes, reserving juice. Bring juice to boil in large saucepan. Add onion and garlic. Reduce heat and simmer until onion is tender, about 15 minutes. Add porcini, reserved porcini liquid, tomatoes, olives and next 6 ingredients. Partially cover pot and simmer sauce until thickened slightly, about 30 minutes. Season sauce to taste with salt and pepper.

Cook pasta in large pot of boiling salted water until just tender but still firm to bite. Drain pasta. Return to pot. Add sauce to pasta. Toss to blend and serve.

Porcini mushrooms are available at Italian markets, specialty foods stores and many supermarkets.

**Small brine-cured black olives, available at specialty foods stores and in some supermarkets.*

4 SERVINGS

◆ ◆ ◆

PASTA SUPPER FOR FOUR

LOX AND MELON WITH
CHIVES AND LEMON
(PAGE 13)

FUSILLI WITH PORCINI
PUTTANESCA SAUCE
(AT LEFT; PICTURED AT LEFT)

ROASTED FENNEL AND
PEAR SALAD WITH
BALSAMIC-PEAR DRESSING
(PAGE 159)

PINOT GRIGIO

THREE-CITRUS MERINGUE TART
(PAGE 176)

◆ ◆ ◆

Pizza with Fontina, Pepperoni and Tomatoes

◆ ◆ ◆

1   12-inch-diameter baked cheese pizza crust (such as Boboli)
8   ounces Fontina cheese, grated (about 2 cups packed)
2½   ounces pepperoni, thinly sliced
4   large plum tomatoes, chopped (about 1½ cups)
2   tablespoons chopped fresh sage or 1½ teaspoons
      dried rubbed sage
½   teaspoon dried crushed red pepper

Preheat oven to 450°F. Place crust on large baking sheet. Sprinkle Fontina over. Arrange pepperoni atop cheese. Sprinkle tomatoes, sage and red pepper over pizza. Season lightly with salt.

Bake pizza until crust is golden and cheese melts, about 15 minutes. Cool in pan 5 minutes. Cut into wedges.

MAKES 1 LARGE PIZZA

Pizza with Caramelized Onions, Blue Cheese and Mushrooms

◆ ◆ ◆

2½   tablespoons olive oil
2   large onions, thinly sliced (about 5 cups)
2   teaspoons brown sugar

8   ounces fresh shiitake mushrooms, stemmed, caps sliced
1   12-inch-diameter baked cheese pizza crust (such as Boboli)
8   ounces blue cheese, crumbled
1   tablespoon chopped fresh thyme or 1 teaspoon dried

Heat 1 tablespoon oil in large nonstick skillet over medium heat. Add onions and sauté until tender, about 10 minutes. Sprinkle brown sugar over onions. Reduce heat to medium-low; sauté until onions are golden brown, about 20 minutes.

Heat 1½ tablespoons oil in large skillet over high heat. Add mushrooms; sauté until tender and golden, about 8 minutes. Season with salt and pepper. *(Onions and mushrooms can be prepared 1 day ahead. Cover separately and refrigerate.)*

PIZZA PARTY FOR SIX

ARTICHOKE BOTTOMS WITH
CRÈME FRAÎCHE AND CAVIAR
(PAGE 24)

PIZZA WITH FETA, TOMATOES,
OLIVES AND SHRIMP
(OPPOSITE; PICTURED ABOVE)

PIZZA WITH FONTINA,
PEPPERONI AND TOMATOES
(AT RIGHT; PICTURED ABOVE)

PIZZA WITH CARAMELIZED
ONIONS, BLUE CHEESE
AND MUSHROOMS
(AT RIGHT; PICTURED ABOVE)

ARUGULA SALAD

CHIANTI

COFFEE ICE CREAM SUNDAES

◆ ◆ ◆

Preheat oven to 450°F. Place pizza crust on large baking sheet. Sprinkle blue cheese and thyme over pizza crust. Top with onions. Sprinkle mushrooms over onions.

Bake pizza until cheese melts, about 15 minutes. Cool pizza in pan 5 minutes. Cut into wedges.

MAKES 1 LARGE PIZZA

Pizza with Feta, Tomatoes, Olives and Shrimp

◆ ◆ ◆

1   12-inch-diameter baked cheese pizza crust (such as Boboli)
8   ounces mozzarella cheese, grated (about 2 cups packed)
1   pound plum tomatoes, thinly sliced
8   ounces feta cheese, crumbled
16 brine-cured black olives (such as Kalamata), pitted
½   cup chopped green onions (green part only)
2   tablespoons chopped fresh oregano or 2 teaspoons dried

½   pound cooked peeled large shrimp

Preheat oven to 450°F. Place pizza crust on large baking sheet. Sprinkle mozzarella cheese over. Arrange tomatoes atop cheese. Sprinkle feta cheese over tomatoes. Sprinkle olives, ⅓ cup green onions and oregano over pizza.

Bake pizza 10 minutes. Remove pizza from oven. Arrange shrimp atop pizza. Continue baking until crust is golden and mozzarella melts, about 4 minutes longer. Cool pizza in pan 5 minutes. Sprinkle remaining green onions over pizza. Cut into wedges.

MAKES 1 LARGE PIZZA

A purchased baked cheese pizza crust is a delicious alternative to making your own dough. This Greek-inspired pie is prepared with robust Mediterranean ingredients—tomatoes, feta cheese, olives and oregano.

◆ ◆ ◆

Grilled Rosemary-crusted Pizzas with Sausage, Peppers and Cheese

◆ ◆ ◆

To test that the dough has risen sufficiently, push two fingers into it. The depressions should remain.

To prevent the dough from sticking as you stretch it into a nine-inch round, use flour sparingly; too much will result in a tough crust.

The first grilled side of the pizza becomes the surface that will hold the toppings. Grill each dough round until the top puffs slightly and the bottom is golden brown and crisp.

DOUGH

1	cup warm water (105°F to 115°F)
1	tablespoon sugar
1	envelope dry yeast
3	tablespoons olive oil
3	cups (or more) all purpose flour
1½	teaspoons salt
1	tablespoon chopped fresh rosemary

TOPPINGS

¾	cup olive oil
6	tablespoons balsamic vinegar
3	tablespoons minced garlic
2	tablespoons chopped fresh rosemary
1	pound spicy Italian sausages
2	yellow or red bell peppers, cored, quartered lengthwise
1	large red onion, peeled, cut through root end into ½-inch-thick wedges
2	cups grated mozzarella cheese
½	cup freshly grated Parmesan cheese
2	cups crumbled chilled soft fresh goat cheese (such as Montrachet)
4	plum tomatoes, halved, seeded, chopped
¾	cup chopped green onion tops

FOR DOUGH: Combine water and sugar in processor. Sprinkle yeast over; let stand until foamy, about 10 minutes. Add oil, then 3 cups flour and salt. Process until dough forms, about 1 minute. Turn dough out onto floured work surface. Sprinkle with rosemary. Knead until dough is smooth and elastic, adding more flour by tablespoonfuls if dough is sticky, about 5 minutes. Lightly oil large bowl. Add dough; turn to coat with oil. Cover with plastic, then towel. Let stand in warm draft-free area until dough doubles, about 1 hour.

Punch down dough. Knead in bowl 2 minutes.

FOR TOPPINGS: Whisk first 4 ingredients in medium bowl. Let vinaigrette stand 15 minutes at room temperature or chill 2 hours.

Prepare barbecue (medium heat). Arrange Italian sausages, peppers and onion on baking sheet. Brush with some of vinaigrette. Sprinkle with salt and pepper. Grill sausages until cooked

Bon Appétit: The Flavors of 1998

through and peppers and onion until slightly charred and crisp-tender, turning and basting occasionally, about 12 minutes for sausages and 8 minutes for peppers and onion.

Transfer sausages and vegetables to cutting board. Cut sausages into ½-inch pieces and peppers into thin strips.

Add coals to barbecue, if necessary. Divide dough into 4 equal pieces. Stretch out each piece on floured surface to 9-inch round.

Place 2 dough rounds on grill. Grill over medium heat until top of dough puffs and underside is crisp, about 3 minutes. Turn rounds over. Grill 1 minute. Transfer to baking sheet with well-grilled side up. Repeat with remaining 2 dough rounds. Sprinkle each with ¼ of mozzarella and Parmesan. Top each with ¼ of sausage, peppers and onion, then with ¼ of goat cheese, tomatoes and green onions. Drizzle each with 1½ tablespoons vinaigrette.

Using large metal spatula, return 2 pizzas to grill. Close grill or cover pizzas loosely with foil. Grill until cheeses melt and dough is cooked through and browned, using tongs to rotate pizzas for even cooking, about 5 minutes. Transfer to plates. Repeat grilling for remaining 2 pizzas and serve.

MAKES FOUR 8-INCH PIZZAS

·ON THE SIDE·

Clockwise from bottom left: Crostini with Spiced Crab and Shrimp Salad (page 23); Roasted Salmon with Salsa Verde (page 96); White Chocolate and Summer Berry Napoleons (page 202); and Bulgur, Cucumber, Dill and Mint Salad (page 161).

◆ SIDE DISHES ◆

Succotash

◆ ◆ ◆

4	ears fresh corn
3	cups chicken stock or canned low-salt broth
7	bacon slices, chopped
½	cup finely chopped shallots
¼	cup finely chopped carrot
¼	cup finely chopped celery
1	Yukon Gold potato, cut into ½-inch pieces
½	cup chopped red bell pepper
¼	cup whipping cream
8	ounces green beans, cut into ½-inch pieces
½	cup frozen lima beans, thawed

Chopped fresh parsley

Cut enough kernels from corncobs to measure 3 cups; reserve cobs. Bring 3 cups chicken stock to boil in heavy large saucepan. Add corncobs. Boil until stock is reduced by half, about 15 minutes. Discard corncobs. Set stock aside.

Sauté bacon in heavy large skillet over medium heat until brown and crisp, about 5 minutes. Add shallots, carrot and celery to skillet; sauté until tender, about 5 minutes. Stir in potato, bell pepper, cream and reduced stock. Cover and cook until potato is tender, about 10 minutes. Add green beans, lima beans and 3 cups corn kernels. Cover and cook until green beans and lima beans are tender, about 5 minutes. Uncover and cook until liquid thickens, about 2 minutes. Season to taste with salt and pepper.

Transfer succotash to serving bowl. Garnish with parsley.

6 SERVINGS

◆ ◆ ◆

Lima beans, corn, bacon and bell peppers go into this popular southern side dish. The name succotash comes from the Naragansett Indian word *msickquatash*, which means "boiled whole kernels of corn."

◆ ◆ ◆

Oven-roasted Vegetables with Fresh Herbs

◆ ◆ ◆

2   tablespoons chopped fresh parsley
2   tablespoons chopped fresh cilantro
2   tablespoons chopped fresh basil
1   small garlic clove, minced

    Nonstick vegetable oil spray
12   asparagus spears, trimmed
1   medium zucchini, trimmed, cut into ½-inch-thick diagonal slices
1   medium-size yellow crookneck squash, trimmed, cut into ½-inch-thick diagonal slices
1   red bell pepper, quartered, seeded
2   teaspoons olive oil

Combine parsley, cilantro, basil and garlic in small bowl.

Preheat oven to 425°F. Spray large baking sheet (preferably nonstick) with vegetable oil spray. Combine vegetables in large bowl. Drizzle oil over and toss to coat. Arrange vegetables in single layer on prepared baking sheet. Roast 15 minutes. Turn zucchini and yellow squash over and roast until tender and golden, about 5 minutes longer. Transfer asparagus, zucchini and yellow squash to platter; cover with foil. Turn bell pepper over; roast until slightly charred and tender, about 15 minutes longer.

Transfer pepper to platter with other vegetables. Sprinkle with herb mixture. Season with salt and pepper. Serve warm, or let stand up to 4 hours and serve at room temperature.

4 SERVINGS

Grilled Asparagus

◆ ◆ ◆

1½   pounds asparagus, trimmed
    Nonstick olive oil spray

Prepare barbecue (medium-high heat). Lightly spray asparagus with olive oil spray. Grill asparagus until tender and beginning to brown, turning frequently, about 5 minutes. Transfer to platter. Sprinkle with salt to taste. Serve warm or at room temperature.

6 SERVINGS

◆ ◆ ◆

Asparagus is enhanced only by a little olive-oil cooking spray and salt in a simple, sensational side dish that is low in calories, cholesterol and fat.

◆ ◆ ◆

Green Beans with
Toasted Pine Nut Oil

◆ ◆ ◆

3   pounds green beans, trimmed

1   cup pine nuts, toasted

6   tablespoons olive oil

Cook beans in large pot of boiling salted water until crisp-tender, about 5 minutes. Drain. Rinse with cold water to cool. Drain well. Transfer beans to large bowl. Set aside.

Coarsely grind pine nuts in processor. Transfer to medium bowl. Mix in oil. *(Beans and oil can be prepared 1 day ahead. Cover beans; chill. Cover oil and let stand at room temperature. Let beans stand 2 hours at room temperature before continuing.)*

Add pine nut oil to beans; toss. Season with salt and pepper.

12 SERVINGS

Mixed Vegetable Sauté with Ginger

◆ ◆ ◆

1 cup thin diagonal carrot slices
1 cup matchstick-size strips red bell pepper
1 cup thinly sliced zucchini
1 cup thinly sliced yellow crookneck squash

1 teaspoon oriental sesame oil
2 tablespoons minced peeled fresh ginger
1 tablespoon reduced-sodium soy sauce
¼ cup chopped fresh chives

Arrange carrot, bell pepper, zucchini and squash on large microwave-safe plate. Cover plate tightly with plastic wrap. Microwave on high until vegetables begin to soften, about 1½ minutes.

Heat oil in large nonstick skillet over medium-high heat. Add ginger; stir 30 seconds. Add vegetables; sauté until crisp-tender, about 2 minutes. Sprinkle with soy sauce; season with salt and pepper. Mix in chives. Transfer vegetables to bowl and serve.

4 SERVINGS

◆ ◆ ◆

In an interesting, timesaving technique, the vegetables are microwaved just until they begin to soften; then they are quickly sautéed in a small amount of oriental sesame oil.

◆ ◆ ◆

White Bean Ragout with Lemon Oil and Shiitake Mushrooms

◆ ◆ ◆

2 cups dried Great Northern beans (about 13 ounces)

8 cups water
1 onion, cut into 8 wedges
3 bay leaves

½ cup extra-virgin olive oil
12 ¼-inch-thick lemon slices

8 ounces fresh shiitake mushrooms, stemmed, caps sliced
3 tablespoons chopped fresh parsley
3 tablespoons chopped fresh thyme or 1 tablespoon dried
3 tablespoons chopped chives or green onions
3 tablespoons fresh lemon juice

2 cups chopped seeded tomatoes
½ cup grated Parmesan cheese (about 1½ ounces)

Place beans in large pot. Add enough cold water to cover beans by 3 inches; let stand overnight. Drain.

Return beans to pot. Add 8 cups water, onion and bay leaves. Bring to boil. Reduce heat; cover and simmer until beans are tender, stirring occasionally, about 1 hour. Reserve 1 cup cooking liquid. Drain beans; transfer to baking pan. Discard onion and bay leaves.

Meanwhile, combine oil and lemon slices in heavy medium saucepan. Simmer over low heat until lemon slices are translucent, about 5 minutes. Let cool uncovered 30 minutes. Strain lemon oil into bowl. Transfer 4 lemon slices to plate; cut in half and reserve (discard remaining lemon slices). *(Beans, cooking liquid, lemon oil and lemons can be prepared 1 day ahead. Chill separately.)*

Heat 4 tablespoons lemon oil in heavy large pot over medium-high heat. Add mushrooms and sauté until brown and tender, about 5 minutes. Add beans, 1 cup reserved cooking liquid, remaining lemon oil, herbs and lemon juice to mushrooms. Simmer over medium heat 5 minutes to blend flavors. Cool completely.

Stir chopped tomatoes and grated Parmesan cheese into bean mixture. Season to taste with salt and pepper. Spoon bean mixture onto platter. Garnish with halved lemon slices.

8 SERVINGS

◆ ◆ ◆

This hearty side dish combines Great Northern Beans (which are similar in shape to lima beans but have a more delicate flavor), meaty shiitake mushrooms, fresh herbs and lemon oil, which is made by simmering lemon slices in olive oil.

◆ ◆ ◆

Spring Peas with Lettuce and Mint

◆ ◆ ◆

½   cup canned low-salt chicken broth
1   10-ounce package frozen peas, thawed
1   cup thinly sliced romaine lettuce
3   tablespoons chopped fresh mint

Bring broth to boil in medium saucepan. Add peas and simmer until heated through, about 4 minutes. Stir in lettuce and mint. Season to taste with salt and serve.

4 SERVINGS

Baked Polenta with Garlic

◆ ◆ ◆

2¾   cups canned low-salt chicken broth
2   cups water
1½   cups milk
3   garlic cloves, minced
1½   teaspoons chopped fresh rosemary
½   teaspoon salt
1½   cups yellow cornmeal
8   tablespoons grated Parmesan cheese (about 1½ ounces)

Preheat oven to 375°F. Butter 2-quart soufflé dish. Bring first 6 ingredients to boil in heavy large saucepan. Gradually add cornmeal, whisking until smooth. Reduce heat to low; cook until cornmeal is very soft and mixture is thick and creamy, stirring occasionally, about 12 minutes. Remove from heat; stir in 6 tablespoons Parmesan cheese. Season with pepper.

Transfer to prepared dish. Sprinkle 2 tablespoons Parmesan over polenta. *(Can be made 1 day ahead. Cool. Cover and chill.)*

Bake polenta until heated through and golden on top, about 30 minutes. Serve polenta warm.

6 SERVINGS

◆ ◆ ◆

Polenta is often made at the last minute on the stove. Since this garlic- and Parmesan-flavored version is baked, it's a great do-ahead dish.

◆ ◆ ◆

Mashed Potatoes with Black Olives

◆ ◆ ◆

3½   pounds red-skinned potatoes, peeled, cut into 1-inch pieces
⅔   cup milk
4½   tablespoons butter
⅔   cup chopped pitted brine-cured black olives (such as Kalamata)
2   tablespoons chopped Italian parsley
3   tablespoons olive oil

Cook potatoes in large pot of boiling salted water until very tender, about 15 minutes. Drain. Transfer potatoes to large mixing bowl. Add milk and butter. Using electric mixer, beat until potatoes are smooth. Stir in olives. Season with salt and pepper. Transfer to serving bowl. Sprinkle with parsley; drizzle oil over.

6 SERVINGS

Sweet Potato Gratin with Ginger

◆ ◆ ◆

4½   pounds tan-skinned sweet potatoes, peeled, thinly sliced
1½   pounds red-skinned sweet potatoes (yams), peeled, thinly sliced
⅓   cup finely chopped shallots
1   tablespoon (generous) minced crystallized ginger
1   cup whipping cream
1   cup canned low-salt chicken broth
2   tablespoons (¼ stick) butter, melted
¼   teaspoon ground nutmeg

Chopped fresh parsley

Preheat oven to 400°F. Butter 15 x 10-inch baking dish. Arrange ⅓ of both potatoes in dish. Sprinkle with half of shallots and ginger. Sprinkle with salt and pepper. Cover with ⅓ of both potatoes. Sprinkle with remaining shallots and ginger. Cover with remaining potatoes. Mix cream and broth and pour over. Brush potatoes with melted butter. Sprinkle with ground nutmeg.

Cover potatoes with foil. Bake 45 minutes. Uncover; bake until potatoes are tender and liquid thickens, about 15 minutes. Cool gratin 10 minutes. Top with parsley.

10 SERVINGS

ONE POTATO, TWO...

Of all vegetables, potatoes are surely the most popular. Mashed, fried, baked, boiled or roasted, they're delicious every which way. And as familiar as they are, there is surprising variety among them.

◆ Russet: Also called an Idaho potato or baking potato. With its long, slightly oval shape and rough, brown skin, the russet has white, flaky flesh and a high-starch content, which makes it ideal for baking, mashing or frying.

◆ Long White: Also called White Rose or California Long White. Similar in shape to the russet but with pale tan skin, the Long White is a good all-purpose potato for baking, boiling or frying.

◆ Round White and Round Red: Also known as boiling potatoes. Both kinds have waxy flesh with a low starch content; they're great for mashing, roasting and frying.

◆ Sweet Potato: Although not technically a member of the potato family (it's a root vegetable native to tropical areas of the Americas), the pale-skinned sweet potato and the darker-skinned variety, often called a yam, are used in cooking much the same way a potato is.

◆ ◆ ◆

EXPERTS AND THEIR GADGETS

Of all the items in your kitchen, what's the one thing that you just can't do without? We asked 10 international food experts that very question, and each had a quick answer.

◆ Blender: Pierre Hermé, vice president and executive pastry chef, Ladurée, Paris.

◆ Cleaver: Nina Simonds, Chinese food expert, teacher and author, Massachusetts.

◆ Espresso Machine: Christopher Gross, chef/owner Christopher's and Christopher's Bistro, Phoenix.

◆ Frying Pan: Julia Child, cookbook author and television personality, Massachusetts.

◆ Heavy-duty Mixer: François Payard, executive pastry chef and co-owner of Payard, New York.

◆ Hot-Water Tap: Patrick O'Connell, chef and co-owner of The Inn at Little Washington, Virginia.

◆ Mortar and Pestle: Diana Kennedy, cookbook author and Mexican food expert, Mexico.

◆ Sauce Whisk: Richard Melman, founder and president of Lettuce Entertain You, Chicago.

◆ Toaster Oven: Wolfgang Puck, chef and restaurateur, Los Angeles.

◆ Wine Opener: Rusty Staub, wine connoisseur, collector, New York.

◆ ◆ ◆

Grilled New Potatoes with Parmesan and Herbs

◆ ◆ ◆

3	pounds small red-skinned potatoes
4	tablespoons olive oil
1	cup thinly sliced green onions
3	tablespoons chopped Italian parsley
3	tablespoons grated Parmesan
3	garlic cloves, finely chopped
2	teaspoons chopped fresh oregano

Cook potatoes in large pot of boiling salted water until tender, about 15 minutes. Drain potatoes; cool.

Prepare barbecue (medium heat). Cut potatoes in half; transfer to large bowl. Add 2 tablespoons oil; toss to coat. Grill potatoes until golden, turning occasionally, about 5 minutes. Transfer to bowl. Drizzle 2 tablespoons oil over. Add remaining ingredients; toss to coat. Season with salt and pepper. Serve warm.

8 SERVINGS

Mashed Potatoes with Cilantro and Roasted Chilies

◆ ◆ ◆

2	poblano chilies*
4	pounds russet potatoes (about 6 large), peeled, quartered
3	garlic cloves, peeled, bruised
1	cup warm half and half
¼	cup (½ stick) butter, room temperature
¼	cup chopped fresh cilantro

Char poblano chilies over gas flame or in broiler until blackened on all sides. Wrap in paper bag and let stand 10 minutes. Peel and seed chilies; chop coarsely.

Cook potatoes and garlic in large pot of boiling salted water until very tender, about 35 minutes. Drain. Transfer potatoes and garlic to bowl. Using electric mixer, beat until mixture is smooth. Gradually beat in half and half. Add butter and beat until melted. Stir in chilies and cilantro. Season with salt and pepper.

A fresh green chili, often called a pasilla, *available at Latin American markets and some supermarkets.*

8 SERVINGS

Roasted Jumbo French Fries

◆ ◆ ◆

4   large long russet potatoes (about 14 ounces each), unpeeled
⅔   cup olive oil

Preheat oven to 400°F. Rinse potatoes thoroughly with cold water; wipe dry. Cut each potato lengthwise into quarters. Combine potatoes and olive oil in large bowl; toss to coat well. Arrange potato quarters, 1 flat side down, on baking sheet. Bake 30 minutes. Using metal spatula, turn potatoes onto second flat side. Continue to bake until potatoes are tender and deep brown, about 30 minutes longer. Season potatoes with salt and pepper. Serve hot.

4 SERVINGS

Potato and Parmesan Gratin

◆ ◆ ◆

2½   pounds russet potatoes, peeled, cut into ⅛-inch-thick slices
¼   cup (½ stick) butter, melted
2   cups (packed) freshly grated Parmesan cheese (about 10 ounces)
2   cups milk (do not use low-fat or nonfat)

Preheat oven to 400°F. Butter 13 x 9 x 2-inch glass baking dish. Layer ⅓ of potatoes evenly in prepared dish. Sprinkle with salt and pepper. Drizzle with ⅓ of melted butter. Top with ⅓ of Parmesan cheese. Repeat layering twice more with remaining potatoes, butter and Parmesan cheese. Pour milk evenly over.

Bake potatoes 15 minutes. Reduce temperature to 350°F. Continue to bake until potatoes are tender, top is golden brown and most of milk is absorbed, about 1 hour longer. Remove from oven; let gratin stand 10 minutes and serve.

6 SERVINGS

Here's a simple recipe for home-made French fries. They're great as a go-with for burgers or sandwiches—or even on their own as a tasty snack.

◆ ◆ ◆

Crispy Garlic Risotto Cakes

◆ ◆ ◆

14 whole garlic cloves, unpeeled
2   teaspoons olive oil

4   cups water

4   tablespoons (½ stick) butter
¼   cup finely chopped onion
1   cup arborio rice*
½   cup dry white wine

¼   cup freshly grated Parmesan cheese
2   tablespoons chopped fresh parsley

All purpose flour

Preheat oven to 375°F. Toss garlic with 2 teaspoons oil in small baking dish. Cover with aluminum foil. Bake until garlic is tender, about 30 minutes. Uncover; bake until garlic is very tender, about 10 minutes longer. Cool garlic; peel. Puree half of garlic in processor. Thinly slice remaining garlic. Set garlic puree and slices aside.

Bring 4 cups water to simmer in medium saucepan. Reduce heat to low, cover and keep hot.

Melt 2 tablespoons butter in heavy large saucepan over medium-high heat. Add chopped onion and sauté until tender, about 3 minutes. Add rice and stir until golden, about 3 minutes. Add wine and stir until absorbed, about 2 minutes. Add 1 cup hot water. Adjust heat so that liquid bubbles gently. Stir until liquid is absorbed. Continue adding hot water 1 cup at a time until rice is just tender and mixture is very thick, simmering until liquid is absorbed before each addition and stirring frequently, about 25 minutes. Transfer risotto to large bowl. Cool 30 minutes.

Mix cheese, parsley and garlic puree and slices into risotto. Season to taste with salt and pepper. Cover; chill until cold, 2 hours.

Shape risotto into six 3-inch-diameter patties, ¾ inch thick, using about ⅓ cup risotto for each. Place risotto cakes on large baking sheet. Cover and refrigerate 1 hour. *(Risotto cakes can be prepared 8 hours ahead. Keep refrigerated.)*

◆ ◆ ◆

Skillet cakes made from grains were popular this year at restaurants across the country. This recipe has a great do-ahead hint—the rice cakes can be prepared eight hours before they're cooked. And they are a good way to use leftover risotto.

◆ ◆ ◆

Place flour in shallow dish. Lightly coat each risotto cake with flour. Melt 1 tablespoon butter in heavy large skillet over medium heat. Add 3 risotto cakes; cook until golden brown and heated through, about 3 minutes per side. Transfer to plate lined with paper towels to drain. Repeat with remaining 1 tablespoon butter and 3 risotto cakes. Transfer risotto cakes to platter and serve.

Arborio is an Italian short-grain rice available at Italian markets and many supermarkets.

6 SERVINGS

Rice with Wild Mushrooms and Chives

◆ ◆ ◆

6   tablespoons (¾ stick) butter
2   cups long-grain white rice
3½   cups canned low-salt chicken broth

12   ounces fresh wild mushrooms (such as morels, chanterelles or stemmed shiitakes), coarsely chopped

⅓   cup chopped fresh chives

Melt 2 tablespoons butter in heavy large saucepan over medium-high heat. Add rice; stir to coat. Add broth and bring to boil. Reduce heat to low, cover and cook until all liquid is absorbed and rice is tender, about 20 minutes. Remove from heat. Let stand covered for 5 minutes. Season with salt and pepper.

Meanwhile, melt 4 tablespoons butter in large skillet over medium-high heat. Add wild mushrooms; sauté until tender, about 5 minutes. Season with salt and pepper.

Transfer rice to large bowl. Add wild mushrooms and chopped fresh chives and toss to combine; serve.

6 SERVINGS

◆ ◆ ◆

To store fresh wild mushrooms, arrange them in a single layer on a paper plate and cover with a damp paper towel. Before using, wipe the mushrooms with another damp towel and dry thoroughly. It is best not to soak them in water as this can make the mushrooms mushy.

◆ ◆ ◆

◆ SALADS ◆

Green Salad with Asparagus, Oranges and Red Onion

◆ ◆ ◆

DRESSING

⅔ cup regular or low-fat mayonnaise

½ cup buttermilk

3 tablespoons chopped fresh basil

2 tablespoons olive oil (preferably extra-virgin)

2 tablespoons white wine vinegar

2 tablespoons chopped fresh tarragon

SALAD

24 asparagus spears, trimmed

4 oranges

12 cups mixed baby greens

1 tablespoon chopped fresh basil

1 tablespoon chopped fresh tarragon

½ cup thinly sliced red onion

FOR DRESSING: Whisk mayonnaise, buttermilk, basil, oil, vinegar and tarragon in medium bowl to blend. Chill until cold.

FOR SALAD: Cook asparagus in large pot of boiling salted water until crisp-tender, about 2 minutes. Transfer asparagus to bowl of ice water to cool. Drain thoroughly.

Cut peel and white pith from oranges. Using small sharp knife, cut between membranes to release orange segments. *(Dressing, asparagus and orange segments can be prepared 1 day ahead. Cover separately and refrigerate.)*

Arrange asparagus spears in sunburst pattern on platter. Place orange segments between asparagus spears. Mound mixed greens in center of serving platter. Sprinkle salad with chopped fresh basil and tarragon. Top with red onion slices. Drizzle some dressing over salad. Pass remaining dressing separately.

8 SERVINGS

The asparagus spears and orange segments are arranged in a sunburst pattern on a large platter, with baby greens, fresh herbs and sliced red onion placed in the center.

◆ ◆ ◆

Salad with Macadamia Nuts and Goat Cheese

◆ ◆ ◆

2   3½-ounce logs soft fresh goat cheese (such as Montrachet), chilled
½   cup chopped macadamia nuts

8   cups mixed baby greens
1   avocado, peeled, halved, pitted, cut into thin wedges
8   tablespoons olive oil
3   tablespoons balsamic vinegar

Cut each goat cheese log crosswise into 6 rounds. Place macadamia nuts in shallow bowl. Press cheese rounds into nuts, turning to coat. Arrange cheese rounds on plate; reserve any remaining nuts. Cover cheese and refrigerate.

Mound greens in large salad bowl. Arrange avocado wedges atop greens. Whisk 6 tablespoons olive oil and vinegar in small bowl to blend. Season dressing to taste with salt and pepper.

Heat 2 tablespoons oil in heavy large skillet over medium heat. Add cheese rounds; sauté until just warmed through but still holding shape, about 1 minute per side. Arrange rounds on top of salad. Drizzle dressing over; sprinkle with reserved nuts and serve.

4 SERVINGS

ABOUT GOAT CHEESE

Goat cheese could be the cheese of the nineties. It's low in fat yet there is no shortchanging on flavor.

All goat's milk cheeses are characterized by their tangy taste, which can vary from mildly tangy to pungent based on how long the cheese is aged. The longer the aging, the stronger the flavor (and the firmer the texture). Here's a mild-to-strong list of some of the more unique goat cheeses available in specialty foods stores.

◆ Fromage Blanc: This soft and mildly flavored cheese, often sold in pints, is aged for only one day.

◆ Chabis: Generally cylindrical in shape, chabis is aged less than a week and has a mild flavor and texture similar to cream cheese.

◆ Bûche: These cheese logs are aged one week or more and have a firm but smooth texture, like butter. They are often rolled in ashes.

◆ Cabécou: Firm and nut-flavored, these cute little buttons of cheese (weighing in at one ounce each) are aged 10 days. They are delicious marinated in olive oil and herbs.

◆ Crottin: Aged two to three weeks, this semi-hard cheese is also available in small round buttons. It has a somewhat stronger flavor than other goat cheeses.

◆ ◆ ◆

ABOUT BEETS

Native to the Mediterranean region, beets are thought to date back to the prehistoric era. Romans ate only the leaves for hundreds of years before they finally discovered how good the root tasted when cooked.

And if you've only ever tried canned beets, you too may be surprised by the wonderful flavor and texture of fresh beets.

When shopping for fresh beets, choose those that are small to medium in size, with smooth, unblemished skins and crisp bright green leaves. At home, remove the greens, leaving one to two inches of stem attached to prevent any loss of nutrients during cooking. Store fresh beets in a plastic bag in the refrigerator up to three weeks. The washed and dried beet greens can be refrigerated in a plastic bag for up to three days.

Beets taste great roasted, steamed or boiled. Generally, it's best to peel them after cooking, when the beet skins simply slip off.

A final note: If you want to avoid turning an entire dish that famous beet red, be sure to add beets last when mixing them with other vegetables.

◆ ◆ ◆

Romaine and Roasted-Beet Salad

◆ ◆ ◆

DRESSING

½   cup mayonnaise
1   large shallot, minced
1   tablespoon Sherry wine vinegar
1   large garlic clove, minced
2   teaspoons Dijon mustard
⅓   cup crumbled Roquefort cheese
3   tablespoons whipping cream

SALAD

6   medium beets, tops trimmed

3   hearts of romaine lettuce, quartered lengthwise, ends left intact
1   small red onion, thinly sliced
1   watercress bunch, thick stems trimmed
¾   cup walnut halves, toasted

FOR DRESSING: Whisk first 5 ingredients in small bowl to blend. Fold in Roquefort cheese and cream. Season dressing to taste with salt and pepper. *(Can be prepared 1 day ahead. Cover and refrigerate.)*

FOR SALAD: Preheat oven to 400°F. Wrap beets in foil. Bake until tender, 1 hour 15 minutes. Cool; peel and cut into wedges.

Arrange 2 lettuce quarters crosswise on each of 6 large plates. Surround lettuce with beet wedges. Top with onion slices and watercress. Drizzle with dressing. Sprinkle with walnuts; serve.

6 SERVINGS

Tomato Salad

◆ ◆ ◆

6   large plum tomatoes, each cut into 4 wedges
3   tablespoons extra-virgin olive oil
1   tablespoon balsamic vinegar

Place tomatoes in large bowl. Whisk oil and vinegar in small bowl to blend. Season dressing to taste with salt and pepper. Pour over tomatoes and toss gently to coat.

6 SERVINGS

Eggplant and Watercress Salad with Sesame Seeds

◆ ◆ ◆

1   cup hickory smoke chips, soaked in water 30 minutes, drained
1   large eggplant (about 1¼ pounds), sliced into ¾-inch-thick rounds
4   tablespoons corn oil

1   tablespoon sesame seeds

2   tablespoons seasoned rice vinegar*
1½ teaspoons soy sauce
¾   teaspoon oriental sesame oil
⅛   teaspoon dried crushed red pepper
1   bunch watercress, trimmed

Prepare barbecue (medium heat). Place hickory smoke chips in 8 x 6-inch foil packet with open top. Set packet atop coals about 5 minutes before grilling. Brush eggplant with 2 tablespoons corn oil. Grill until cooked through, about 5 minutes per side. Cut eggplant into ¾-inch cubes. Place in large bowl.

Toast sesame seeds in heavy small skillet over medium-low heat until light brown, about 5 minutes.

Whisk vinegar, soy sauce, sesame oil, crushed red pepper and 2 tablespoons corn oil in medium bowl. Add watercress to eggplant in large bowl. Toss with enough dressing to coat. Season with salt and pepper. Sprinkle sesame seeds over salad.

Also known as sushi vinegar; available at Asian markets and in the Asian foods section of some supermarkets.

4 SERVINGS

◆ ◆ ◆

Watercress enlivens everything it's added to, with its bright color and distinct peppery taste. Here, the green is partnered with grilled eggplant and sesame seeds, and dressed with a blend of seasoned rice vinegar, soy sauce and oriental sesame oil, in a salad with an Asian twist.

◆ ◆ ◆

VINEGAR VARIATIONS

Vinegars may be flavored with fruit, herbs, vegetables, spices or any blend of the bunch. White wine vinegar and Champagne vinegar make neutral slates on which to layer flavors, although red wine vinegar and rice vinegar can also work well.

Making flavored vinegar is a snap, a simple matter of combining a vinegar with the flavoring of choice in a clean glass container with a non-metal lid and letting it steep in a cool dark place until the desired taste is achieved. The flavoring can be left in or strained out, as desired.

Here are a few off-beat combinations you might want to try.

◆ Lemongrass Vinegar: Bruise stalks of lemongrass and steep in rice vinegar for about two weeks.

◆ Rose Petal Vinegar: Combine pesticide-free rose petals and Champagne vinegar; the darker the roses, the more intense the color will be. After about 2 weeks, the vinegar will be ready.

◆ Lemon-Garlic Vinegar: Infuse white wine vinegar with lemon peel and peeled, halved garlic cloves. Steep up to one month.

◆ Mango Vinegar: Soak slices of mango in white wine vinegar for about four weeks.

◆ ◆ ◆

Spinach-Orange Salad

◆ ◆ ◆

½ cup fresh orange juice
¼ cup Sherry wine vinegar
3 tablespoons honey
1 tablespoon fresh lime juice
¾ teaspoon chili powder
¾ cup olive oil

2 6-ounce packages baby spinach
4 oranges, peel and white pith removed, quartered, cut crosswise into ¼-inch-thick slices
2 cups matchstick-size strips peeled jicama
1 avocado, peeled, seeded, cubed
½ cup chopped red onion
¼ cup chopped fresh cilantro

Whisk fresh orange juice, Sherry wine vinegar, honey, fresh lime juice and chili powder in large bowl to blend. Gradually whisk in olive oil. Season dressing to taste with salt and pepper.

Combine remaining ingredients in another large bowl. Toss salad with enough dressing to coat lightly.

8 SERVINGS

Penne, Spinach, Asparagus and Cashew Salad

◆ ◆ ◆

1½ pounds asparagus spears, ends trimmed, cut into 1-inch pieces
1½ pounds penne or rigatoni pasta
1 tablespoon plus ½ cup olive oil

¾ cup sliced green onions
6 tablespoons white wine vinegar
2 tablespoons soy sauce
1 6-ounce package baby spinach
1 cup (about 4½ ounces) salted roasted cashews, coarsely chopped

Cook asparagus in large pot of boiling salted water until just tender, about 3 minutes. Using slotted spoon, transfer asparagus to small bowl. Cool. Add pasta to same pot and cook until just tender but still firm to bite. Drain well. Transfer pasta to very large bowl. Toss with 1 tablespoon oil. Cool.

Blend ½ cup oil, green onions, vinegar and soy sauce in blender until smooth, about 2 minutes. *(Asparagus, pasta and dressing can be made 1 day ahead. Cover separately; chill.)* Pour dressing over pasta. Add asparagus, spinach and nuts; toss. Season with salt and pepper.

12 SERVINGS

Green Bean Caesar Salad

◆ ◆ ◆

1	cup plain nonfat yogurt
1	cup fat-free bottled Italian dressing
4	garlic cloves, chopped
2	tablespoons Dijon mustard
2	teaspoons Worcestershire sauce
1	pound green beans, trimmed, halved
2	heads romaine lettuce, torn into bite-size pieces
2	small heads radicchio, thinly sliced
8	tablespoons grated Parmesan cheese

Combine first 5 ingredients in small bowl; whisk to blend. Season dressing to taste with pepper.

Cook beans in medium pot of boiling salted water until crisp-tender, about 4 minutes. Drain. Rinse with cold water; drain. Combine beans, romaine, radicchio and half of cheese in large bowl. Add dressing and toss to coat. Sprinkle with 4 tablespoons cheese.

8 SERVINGS

This reduced-fat version hits all the flavor notes of the original Caesar. Green beans provide crunch, radicchio adds color, and the entire salad comes together in minutes.

Jicama and Grilled Red Pepper Slaw

◆ ◆ ◆

1	cup hickory smoke chips, soaked in water 30 minutes, drained
8	large green onions, trimmed
4½	tablespoons corn oil
3	large red bell peppers
5	tablespoons fresh orange juice
1½	tablespoons fresh lime juice
1	tablespoon honey
¾	teaspoon ground cumin
1	jicama (about 18 ounces), peeled, cut into matchstick-size strips

Prepare barbecue (medium-high heat). Place smoke chips in 8 x 6-inch foil packet with open top. Set packet atop coals about 5 minutes before grilling. Brush green onions with 1½ tablespoons oil. Grill until lightly browned, turning often, about 4 minutes. Cut onions into ¼-inch pieces. Place in large bowl. Grill bell peppers until lightly charred, turning often, about 10 minutes. Enclose in paper bag; let stand 10 minutes. Peel and seed peppers; cut into ¼-inch-wide strips. Add bell peppers to onions.

Whisk orange juice, lime juice, honey, cumin and 3 tablespoons oil in small bowl. *(Vegetables and dressing can be made 8 hours ahead. Cover separately and refrigerate.)* Add jicama and dressing to grilled vegetables; toss to coat. Season with salt and pepper.

6 SERVINGS

Sweet and crunchy jicama and smoky grill-roasted peppers and green onions combine in this attractive side dish. If you like, grill the vegetables and make the dressing ahead, then toss before serving.

Curly Endive with Toasted Almond Dressing

◆ ◆ ◆

3	tablespoons minced shallots
2	tablespoons red wine vinegar
5	tablespoons extra-virgin olive oil
¼	cup whole almonds, toasted, finely chopped
8	cups bite-size pieces curly endive

Whisk shallots and vinegar in medium bowl. Gradually whisk in olive oil. Whisk in almonds. Season with salt and pepper.

Toss curly endive in large bowl with enough dressing to coat.

6 SERVINGS

Italian-Style Cabbage Salad

◆ ◆ ◆

8 cups thinly sliced red cabbage (about ½ large head)
¼ cup chopped Italian parsley
2 tablespoons drained capers

2 tablespoons olive oil (preferably extra-virgin)
2 tablespoons red wine vinegar
2 tablespoons water
1 tablespoon minced garlic

Combine red cabbage, parsley and capers in large bowl.
Whisk olive oil, red wine vinegar, 2 tablespoons water and garlic in small bowl to blend. Add to cabbage mixture and toss to blend.
Season to taste with salt and pepper. *(Can be prepared up to 3 hours
ahead. Cover with plastic wrap and refrigerate.)*

6 SERVINGS

◆ ◆ ◆

Add canned white tuna (packed in
water) to this simple "slaw" for a
delicious and healthful main course.
(And to make life even easier, pick up
one of those convenient bags of sliced
cabbage available in many markets.)

◆ ◆ ◆

Asian Slaw with Peanuts

◆ ◆ ◆

½   cup vegetable oil
¼   cup rice vinegar
2   tablespoons oriental sesame oil
1½   tablespoons minced peeled fresh ginger
2   teaspoons soy sauce

6   cups thinly sliced Napa cabbage
6   green onions, very thinly sliced
6   ounces snow peas, stringed, thinly sliced lengthwise
1   large red bell pepper, thinly sliced
½   cup roasted peanuts

Whisk first 5 ingredients in medium bowl to blend. Season dressing to taste with salt and pepper.

Mix cabbage and remaining ingredients in large bowl. Toss with enough dressing to coat. Season to taste with salt and pepper. *(Can be made 3 hours ahead. Cover and refrigerate.)*

4 SERVINGS

Warm Red Cabbage Salad with Pancetta and Feta

◆ ◆ ◆

12   very thin pancetta slices, or 6 bacon slices, halved

⅓   cup olive oil
⅓   cup raspberry vinegar
2   tablespoons finely chopped shallots
2   tablespoons honey
1¼   pounds red cabbage, cored, thinly sliced (about 5 cups)

¼   pound feta cheese, crumbled
     Watercress (optional)

Working in batches, sauté pancetta in heavy large skillet over medium heat until pale golden, about 3 minutes. Using slotted spoon, transfer to paper towels.

◆ ◆ ◆

Pancetta is an Italian bacon cured in salt. Available at Italian markets and some specialty foods stores, it can be stored tightly wrapped in the refrigerator up to three weeks or frozen for about six months.

◆ ◆ ◆

Remove skillet from heat. Add oil, vinegar, shallots and honey to drippings in skillet. Bring to boil over medium heat. Add cabbage; sauté until heated through but still crunchy, about 3 minutes.

Transfer salad to plates. Top with pancetta and cheese. Garnish with watercress, if desired, and serve salad warm.

6 SERVINGS

Roasted Fennel and Pear Salad with Balsamic-Pear Dressing

◆ ◆ ◆

2   firm but ripe pears, halved, cored
1   medium fennel bulb (about 8 ounces), cored, quartered
1   teaspoon olive oil
⅓   cup canned low-salt chicken broth

2   tablespoons balsamic vinegar

6   cups (packed) mixed baby greens

Preheat oven to 400°F. Arrange pears, cut side up, in square 8 x 8 x 2-inch glass baking dish; add fennel. Drizzle olive oil and chicken broth over pears and fennel. Roast 10 minutes. Turn pears and fennel over and roast until pears are just tender, about 5 minutes longer. Using slotted spoon, transfer pears to plate. Continue roasting fennel until tender, about 15 minutes longer. Transfer fennel to plate with pears, reserving any cooking liquid. Thinly slice fennel and 2 pear halves lengthwise. Cool completely.

Peel remaining 2 pear halves. Transfer peeled pears to processor. Add reserved cooking liquid and vinegar to processor and blend until very smooth. Season dressing with salt and pepper.

Divide greens among 4 plates. Top with fennel and pear. Drizzle some dressing over. Serve, passing remaining dressing.

4 SERVINGS

Roasting tones down the sharpness of the fennel and enhances the sweetness of the pears in this salad. The pears also combine with balsamic vinegar to make a delicious salad dressing without much added fat.

◆ ◆ ◆

Asiago is a semi-firm Italian cheese made from partially skimmed cow's milk. Mild and a little sweet, it is an ideal accent to the peppery arugula and pears in this delicious salad.

◆ ◆ ◆

Arugula, Pear and Asiago Cheese Salad

◆ ◆ ◆

12 cups loosely packed arugula (about 8 ounces total)

3 tablespoons extra-virgin olive oil

4 pears, peeled, cored, sliced

6 ounces Asiago cheese, grated

3 tablespoons coarsely chopped toasted walnuts

Place arugula on platter. Drizzle with oil. Season with salt and pepper. Toss to coat. Top with pears, then cheese and nuts.

12 SERVINGS

New Potato Salad with Sautéed Onion Vinaigrette

◆ ◆ ◆

2¼ pounds small red-skinned potatoes

1½ tablespoons dry white wine

3 teaspoons olive oil

2 cups chopped onions

3 tablespoons balsamic vinegar

2 tablespoons Dijon mustard

1	teaspoon sugar
8	radishes, trimmed, thinly sliced
4	green onions, thinly sliced
¼	cup chopped fresh parsley
1	large cucumber, peeled, halved lengthwise, seeded, thinly sliced

Cook potatoes in large pot of boiling salted water until tender when pierced with fork, about 15 minutes. Drain well. Cool potatoes until lukewarm. Cut potatoes in half. Place in large bowl. Sprinkle white wine over potatoes. Set aside.

Heat 2 teaspoons oil in large nonstick skillet over medium heat. Add onions and sauté until tender, about 5 minutes. Add vinegar, mustard and sugar to skillet and stir to blend. Pour over potatoes and toss to coat. Add radishes, green onions, parsley and remaining 1 teaspoon oil and toss. Season salad with salt and pepper.

Mound salad on platter. Surround with cucumber slices.

6 SERVINGS

◆ ◆ ◆

The rich flavor of sautéed onions gives this low-fat potato salad dressing high-fat taste. Sliced radishes and cucumber take it out of the ordinary.

◆ ◆ ◆

Bulgur, Cucumber, Dill and Mint Salad

◆ ◆ ◆

2	cups fresh lemon juice
1⅓	cups extra-virgin olive oil
¼	cup minced garlic
2	teaspoons salt
2	cups bulgur*

6	medium cucumbers (about 4 pounds), peeled, seeded, chopped
4	cups chopped fresh parsley
3½	cups chopped green onions
3	cups chopped red bell pepper
1	cup chopped fresh dill
⅔	cup chopped fresh mint

Whisk lemon juice, oil, garlic and salt in very large bowl to blend. Season dressing to taste with pepper. Mix in bulgur.

Mix remaining ingredients in medium bowl. Season with salt and pepper. Spoon atop bulgur (do not mix). Cover and chill overnight or up to 2 days. Toss salad. Transfer to serving bowl.

*Also called cracked wheat, bulgur is available at natural foods stores and most supermarkets across the country.

20 SERVINGS

ABOUT ROSEMARY

Rosemary's potent bouquet may have had something to do with the great faith people have put in its powers throughout history. In ancient Greece, it was associated with memory, and scholars of the day would carry a sprig with them when taking exams. Later, during the Middle Ages, sprigs were tucked under bed pillows to prevent nightmares.

Rosemary also had less abstract uses. There was a time when it was placed throughout houses to rid them of bad air, and rosemary baths were hailed for stimulating the skin and senses. In southern France, during the seventeenth century, the herb was so common in the landscape that bakers used the bushes to heat their ovens.

Today, rosemary is still a popular herb, but is used almost exclusively for culinary purposes. It is added to stews, braises and soups, providing an undertone of flavor throughout the dish. Rosemary also finds its way into roasts and vegetable dishes, especially those with potatoes. Chopped finely, it blends well with other hardy herbs to make an aromatic rub. Currently, one of the most popular uses for the fragrant herb is in breads.

♦ ♦ ♦

Rosemary Bread

♦ ♦ ♦

1½	cups warm water (105°F to 115°F)
2	envelopes dry yeast
1	tablespoon sugar
5	cups (about) bread flour
3	tablespoons olive oil
2	tablespoons chopped fresh rosemary
2½	teaspoons salt

Mix water, yeast and sugar in large bowl. Mix in 1 cup flour. Cover and let stand 1 hour at room temperature.

Mix oil, rosemary and salt into yeast mixture. Mix in enough remaining flour to form soft dough. Turn dough out onto lightly floured surface. Knead until smooth and elastic, adding more flour if dough is sticky, about 8 minutes.

Oil large bowl. Add dough and turn to coat. Cover and let rise in warm draft-free area until doubled, about 1 hour.

Lightly flour 2 baking sheets. Punch dough down. Knead until smooth. Divide in half. Form each half into smooth ball. Transfer to baking sheets. Flatten each ball slightly on sheet. Cover each with dry towel. Let dough rise in warm draft-free area until almost doubled in volume, about 1 hour.

Preheat oven to 400°F. Using knife, cut X in top of each loaf. Bake until brown and loaves sound hollow when tapped on bottom, about 40 minutes. Cool loaves on racks.

MAKES 2 LOAVES

Corn Bread with Basil, Roasted Red Peppers and Monterey Jack Cheese

◆ ◆ ◆

8   tablespoons (1 stick) chilled unsalted butter, cut into ½-inch pieces
1   cup chopped onion

1¾ cups yellow cornmeal
1¼ cups all purpose flour
¼   cup sugar
1   tablespoon baking powder
1½ teaspoons salt
½   teaspoon baking soda
1½ cups buttermilk
3   large eggs
1½ cups (lightly packed) grated Monterey Jack cheese with jalapeños
    (about 6 ounces)
1⅓ cups frozen corn kernels, thawed, drained
½   cup drained chopped roasted red peppers from jar
½   cup chopped fresh basil

Preheat oven to 400°F. Butter 9 x 9 x 2-inch baking pan. Melt 1 tablespoon butter in medium nonstick skillet over medium-low heat. Add onion and sauté until tender, about 10 minutes. Cool.

Mix cornmeal and next 5 ingredients in large bowl. Add 7 tablespoons butter and rub in with fingertips until mixture resembles coarse meal. Whisk buttermilk and eggs in medium bowl to blend. Add buttermilk mixture to dry ingredients and stir until blended. Mix in cheese, corn, red peppers, basil and sautéed onion. Transfer batter to prepared baking pan, smoothing top.

Bake corn bread until golden and tester inserted into center comes out clean, about 45 minutes. Cool 20 minutes in pan on rack. *(Can be prepared 8 hours ahead. Cool completely. Cover loosely with foil and let stand at room temperature. If desired, rewarm in 350°F oven about 10 minutes.)* Cut corn bread into squares.

12 SERVINGS

◆ ◆ ◆

This innovative recipe features Monterey Jack, California's most famous cheese. The cheese was created in the 1890s by a dairyman living in the state's first capital, the coastal town of Monterey. A popular jalapeño-studded version of the cheese is used in this tender bread.

Refrigerator Cumin Rolls

♦ ♦ ♦

1   cup milk

¼   cup warm water (110°F to 115°F)
1   package dry yeast
1   teaspoon plus ¼ cup sugar

3   tablespoons unsalted butter, room temperature
1   teaspoon salt
2   large eggs
3¾   cups (about) all purpose flour

½   cup (1 stick) unsalted butter, melted
1   large egg, beaten to blend (for glaze)
2   tablespoons cumin seeds, toasted

Scald milk in heavy medium saucepan. Cool to 105°F.
Meanwhile, mix ¼ cup warm water, yeast and 1 teaspoon sugar in small bowl. Let stand until foamy, about 10 minutes.
Pour milk into large bowl. Add ¼ cup sugar, 3 tablespoons butter and salt. Stir until butter melts and sugar dissolves. Add yeast mix-

♦ ♦ ♦

You can make the dough for these rolls up to two days ahead, then let it rise in the refrigerator. To toast the cumin seeds, stir them in a small skillet over medium heat until fragrant, about five minutes.

♦ ♦ ♦

ture and 2 eggs; whisk to blend. Mix in 1½ cups flour. Gradually mix in enough remaining flour to form stiff dough. Turn out onto lightly floured surface. Knead until smooth and elastic, about 5 minutes.

Lightly oil large bowl. Add dough, turning to coat. Cover; chill overnight *(Can be made 2 days ahead. Keep chilled.)*

Remove risen dough from refrigerator and let stand in bowl for 2 hours at room temperature.

Lightly butter twenty-four ⅓-cup muffin cups. Punch dough down. Divide in half. Cut each half into 12 equal pieces. Roll each piece into ball. Dip ball into melted butter. Pull and stretch ball into 6- to 8-inch-long rope. Tie into knot. Place in muffin cup. Repeat with remaining dough and butter. Brush rolls with egg glaze. Sprinkle with cumin. Let rise 30 minutes at room temperature.

Preheat oven to 400°F. Bake rolls until lightly brown, about 14 minutes. Remove from muffin cups and serve.

MAKES 24

Cranberry-Nut Muffins

◆ ◆ ◆

2	large eggs
½	cup sugar
½	cup sweetened applesauce
½	cup sour cream
1	teaspoon (packed) grated orange peel
2	cups all purpose flour
2	teaspoons baking powder
½	teaspoon baking soda
¼	teaspoon salt
1	cup dried cranberries
¼	cup chopped walnuts

Preheat oven to 375°F. Line 12 muffin cups with foil muffin liners. Using electric mixer, beat eggs and sugar in large bowl until thick and light, about 5 minutes. Add applesauce, sour cream and orange peel and beat until well blended. Sift flour, baking powder, baking soda and salt over mixture; beat until just blended. Stir in cranberries and walnuts. Divide batter among muffin liners.

Bake muffins until tester inserted into center comes out clean, about 20 minutes. Transfer muffins to rack; cool.

MAKES 12

DRIED FRUITS

Packed with concentrated flavor, fiber and nutritional value, dried fruits are good for snacking and baking; they also add sweetness and texture to cereals, grain dishes, salads, stews and puddings. They can be chopped and added to dishes for texture, or pureed and substituted for cooking oil in baked goods. They can be plumped by soaking overnight in water, liqueur or juice; or simmered in a liquid on top of the stove for 15 minutes or in the microwave for 30 seconds.

Where there used to be just raisins and prunes on the shelves, now there is a variety of dried fruits available.

◆ Apricots: There are number of different types to choose from, including California apricots, which are dark orange, tart and tangy, and Turkish (also called International), which are lighter in color and sweeter.

◆ Berries: Dried cranberries, blueberries and cherries are delicious in breads, cakes, muffins and cookies or in sweet and savory duck, lamb, pork or beef dishes.

◆ Figs: Mission figs are a deep rich purple, while the Calimyrna kind are golden colored. Ounce for ounce, figs have as much or more calcium than milk and are loaded with minerals and fiber.

◆ ◆ ◆

THE CHEESE COURSE

The keys to creating a successful cheese course are quality and variety. Your selection can be based on what's available, whim or the occasion.

A ceramic platter, a flat wicker or wood tray, or even a slab of marble or granite would make a fine serving piece for the cheeses. Use a separate sharp knife for each kind of cheese. Fresh fruit or a mixture of dried fruits and nuts are terrific go-withs, as is a home-baked loaf of bread like the walnut version featured at right.

Here are samples of two-, three- and four-cheese combinations.

TWO CHEESES

◆ All-American: a creamy, crumbly Maytag blue and a firm Dry Jack or semi-firm Vermont Cheddar.

◆ International: a semi-firm Swiss Appenzeller and a rich French triple-cream, such as St. André.

THREE CHEESES

◆ All Italian: Taleggio, Gorgonzola, and aged *pecorino Romano*.

◆ All French: a goat cheese (chèvre); a creamy Reblochon; and a gentle blue like *bleu de Bresse*.

FOUR CHEESES

◆ International: an English blue Cheshire, a caciocavallo from Italy, an Australian cheddar, and a rich *corolle du Poitou* from France.

◆ ◆ ◆

Spicy Cheese Biscuits

◆ ◆ ◆

3½ cups all purpose flour
2 tablespoons baking powder
1 tablespoon sugar
2 teaspoons cayenne pepper
½ teaspoon salt
1 cup grated sharp cheddar cheese
¾ cup grated Romano cheese
⅔ cup chilled vegetable shortening, cut into small pieces
1¼ cups chilled buttermilk

Preheat oven to 450°F. Butter large baking sheet. Sift first 5 ingredients twice into medium bowl. Mix in cheeses. Add shortening; rub in with fingertips until mixture resembles coarse meal. Add buttermilk, stirring until dough begins to form clumps.

Turn dough out onto lightly floured surface; knead gently until smooth, about 8 turns. Roll out dough to ¾-inch thickness. Using 3-inch-diameter biscuit cutter, cut out biscuits. Gather dough scraps; roll out to ¾-inch thickness. Cut out additional biscuits. Transfer biscuits to prepared baking sheet. Bake until puffed and golden brown, about 15 minutes. Serve warm.

MAKES ABOUT 9

Walnut Bread

◆ ◆ ◆

½ cup (1 stick) butter or walnut oil
¾ cup finely chopped onion

2 cups warm milk (105°F to 115°F)
2 tablespoons sugar
2 envelopes dry yeast
2 teaspoons salt
5 cups (about) all purpose flour

¾ cup walnuts, toasted, coarsely chopped (about 3 ounces)

Melt butter in heavy large skillet over medium heat. Add onion and sauté until tender, about 5 minutes. Let onion cool.

Combine milk and sugar in large bowl. Sprinkle yeast over; stir to blend. Let stand until foamy, about 10 minutes. Transfer to processor. Mix in onion mixture, salt and 1 cup flour. Blend in enough remaining flour, 1 cup at a time, to form smooth ball. Transfer dough to floured work surface and knead until smooth and elastic, about 3 minutes. Shape dough into ball.

Butter large bowl. Place dough in bowl; turn to coat. Cover bowl with clean kitchen towel. Let dough rise in warm draft-free area until doubled in volume, about 45 minutes.

Butter heavy large baking sheet. Punch down dough. Turn out onto floured work surface. Sprinkle walnuts over; knead to incorporate. Divide dough in half. Shape each half into 6-inch round loaf. Place dough rounds on prepared baking sheet, spacing 4 inches apart. Flatten slightly. Cover with dry towel. Let rise in warm draft-free area until almost doubled in volume, about 45 minutes.

Preheat oven to 400°F. Bake until loaves sound hollow when tapped on bottom, about 25 minutes. Transfer to racks; cool.

MAKES 2 LOAVES

Low-Fat Banana Bread

◆ ◆ ◆

2	large eggs
¾	cup sugar
1	cup mashed ripe bananas (about 3 medium)
⅓	cup buttermilk
1	tablespoon vegetable oil
1	tablespoon vanilla extract
1¾	cups all purpose flour
2	teaspoons baking powder
½	teaspoon baking soda
½	teaspoon salt

Preheat oven to 325°F. Lightly grease 8½ x 4½ x 2½-inch loaf pan; dust with flour. Using electric mixer, beat eggs and sugar in large bowl until thick and light, about 5 minutes. Mix in mashed bananas, buttermilk, oil and vanilla. Sift flour, baking powder, baking soda and salt over mixture; beat until just blended. Transfer batter to pan.

Bake bread until golden brown on top and tester inserted into center comes out clean, about 1 hour. Turn out onto rack. Cool.

MAKES 1 LOAF

◆ ◆ ◆

In this recipe, buttermilk replaces nearly all of the oil that is typically used in a quick bread. Very ripe bananas will give the best flavor.

◆ ◆ ◆

·DESSERTS·

Clockwise from bottom left:
Chocolate-Espresso Pots
de Crème (page 201);
Chocolate-Almond Soufflé
Torte (page 192).

Banana Cream Pie with Maple Syrup

◆ ◆ ◆

PASTRY

1	cup all purpose flour
½	teaspoon sugar
¼	teaspoon salt
¼	cup (½ stick) chilled unsalted butter, cut into pieces
2	tablespoons chilled solid vegetable shortening, cut into pieces
2	tablespoons plus 1 teaspoon (about) ice water

FILLING

2	cups milk (do not use low-fat or nonfat)
½	cup sugar
½	cup all purpose flour
¼	teaspoon salt
5	large egg yolks
2	tablespoons plus 1 teaspoon pure maple syrup
½	teaspoon vanilla extract
2	firm but ripe bananas

TOPPING

¾	cup sour cream
1	tablespoon sugar
½	teaspoon vanilla extract
1	firm but ripe banana

◆ ◆ ◆

This deliciously down-home cream pie has a rich, short crust, sliced bananas, custard filling flavored with maple syrup and sour cream topping.

◆ ◆ ◆

FOR PASTRY: Mix flour, sugar and salt in large bowl. Add butter and shortening; rub in with fingertips until mixture resembles coarse meal. Using fork, stir in enough water to form moist clumps. Gather dough into ball; flatten into disk. Wrap in plastic; chill 1 hour. *(Can be made 2 days ahead. Keep refrigerated. Soften slightly at room temperature before rolling out.)*

Roll out dough on floured surface to 12-inch round. Transfer to 9-inch-diameter glass pie dish. Fold dough edges over and crimp. Freeze crust until firm, approximately 30 minutes.

Preheat oven to 375°F. Line crust with foil; fill with dried beans or pie weights. Bake until sides are set, about 20 minutes. Remove foil and beans and bake until crust is light golden brown, approximately 15 minutes. Transfer to rack; cool completely.

FOR FILLING: Bring milk to simmer in medium saucepan. Remove from heat. Combine sugar, flour and salt in heavy large saucepan. Gradually add ½ cup milk, whisking until smooth. Whisk in remaining milk. Whisk mixture over medium heat until slightly thickened, about 5 minutes. Remove from heat. Mix yolks in large bowl. Gradually whisk in milk mixture. Return to saucepan and stir over medium-low heat until mixture thickens and candy thermometer registers 160°F, about 8 minutes. Transfer custard to clean bowl. Add maple syrup and vanilla. Chill custard until cool but not set, stirring occasionally, about 25 minutes.

Cut bananas into ¼-inch-thick slices. Arrange banana slices on bottom of pie crust. Spoon custard atop banana slices. Chill pie until custard is set, at least 2 hours.

MEANWHILE, PREPARE TOPPING: Combine sour cream, sugar and vanilla in heavy small saucepan. Stir over low heat until mixture is warm and sugar dissolves, about 4 minutes (do not let mixture boil). Spoon over custard. Chill at least 1 and up to 8 hours. Cut banana into ¼-inch-thick slices. Arrange banana slices atop pie.

6 SERVINGS

Lattice-topped
Strawberry-Rhubarb Pie

❖ ❖ ❖

This pretty pie combines the sweet, tart and spice of strawberries, rhubarb and cinnamon. It's topped with a delicate, flaky crust that is arranged in a lattice pattern for an impressive presentation.

CRUST

3	cups all purpose flour
2½	teaspoons sugar
¾	teaspoon salt
⅔	cup chilled solid vegetable shortening, cut into pieces
½	cup plus 2 tablespoons chilled unsalted butter, cut into pieces
10	tablespoons (about) ice water

FILLING

3½	cups ½-inch-thick slices trimmed rhubarb (1½ pounds untrimmed)
1	16-ounce container strawberries, hulled, halved (about 3½ cups)
½	cup (packed) golden brown sugar
½	cup sugar
¼	cup cornstarch
1	teaspoon ground cinnamon
¼	teaspoon salt
1	large egg yolk beaten to blend with 1 teaspoon water (for glaze)

FOR CRUST: Combine flour, sugar and salt in processor. Using on/off turns, cut in shortening and butter until coarse meal forms. Blend in enough ice water 2 tablespoons at a time to form moist clumps. Gather dough into ball; cut in half. Flatten each half into disk. Wrap separately in plastic; refrigerate until firm, about 1 hour.

FOR FILLING: Preheat oven to 400°F. Combine first 7 ingredients in large bowl. Toss gently to blend.

Roll out 1 dough disk on floured work surface to 13-inch round. Transfer to 9-inch-diameter glass pie dish. Trim excess dough, leaving ¾-inch overhang.

Roll out second dough disk on lightly floured surface to 13-inch round. Cut into fourteen ½-inch-wide strips. Spoon filling into crust. Arrange 7 dough strips atop filling, spacing evenly. Form lattice by placing remaining dough strips in opposite direction atop filling. Trim ends of dough strips even with overhang of bottom crust. Fold strip ends and overhang under, pressing to seal. Crimp edges.

Brush glaze over crust. Transfer pie to baking sheet. Bake 20 minutes. Reduce oven temperature to 350°F. Bake pie until crust is golden and filling thickens, about 1 hour 25 minutes. Transfer pie to rack and cool completely.

8 SERVINGS

Chocolate-Orange Tart with Almond Crust

◆ ◆ ◆

CRUST

2   cups whole almonds, toasted

6   tablespoons (packed) golden brown sugar

¼   cup (½ stick) unsalted butter, melted

FILLING

½   cup plus 2 tablespoons whipping cream

6   ounces semisweet chocolate, chopped

2   tablespoons Grand Marnier or other orange liqueur or brandy

⅓   cup orange marmalade

1   ounce (about) white chocolate

FOR CRUST: Preheat oven to 325°F. Finely grind almonds and sugar in processor. Add butter and process until moist clumps form. Press mixture onto bottom and up sides of 9-inch-diameter tart pan with removable bottom. Bake crust until golden brown and firm to touch, about 25 minutes. Cool on rack.

FOR FILLING: Bring cream to simmer in small saucepan. Remove from heat; add semisweet chocolate and whisk until smooth. Whisk in Grand Marnier. Cool until filling begins to thicken but is still pourable, approximately 30 minutes.

Spread marmalade over bottom of crust. Pour chocolate filling over. Refrigerate tart until filling begins to firm but is not quite set, about 20 minutes. Hold white chocolate above tart and scrape with vegetable peeler, allowing chocolate curls to fall onto tart. Chill tart until filling is firm, about 2 hours. *(Can be prepared 1 day ahead. Keep tart refrigerated.)*

8 SERVINGS

◆ ◆ ◆

White chocolate curls make a lovely garnish for this sophisticated dessert. And for a final touch, arrange orange slices on the platter around the tart.

◆ ◆ ◆

Blackberry and Plum Turnovers with Cardamom

◆ ◆ ◆

12 ounces plums, pitted, sliced
2   cups fresh blackberries
½   cup plus 1 tablespoon sugar
⅛   teaspoon ground cardamom
1½ tablespoons cornstarch dissolved in 1½ tablespoons water

1   7-ounce package almond paste
¼   cup whipping cream

1   17¼-ounce package frozen puff pastry (2 sheets), thawed
1   egg, beaten to blend (for glaze)

Combine plums, berries, ½ cup sugar and cardamom in heavy medium saucepan. Bring to boil, stirring. Reduce heat to medium; simmer until plums are soft, about 4 minutes. Add cornstarch mixture and stir until mixture thickens and boils, about 1 minute. Cool. Cover and chill until cold, at least 4 hours or overnight.

Finely grind almond paste in processor. Add whipping cream and puree mixture until smooth.

Line 2 baking sheets with parchment. Roll out 1 pastry sheet on floured surface to 12-inch square. Cut pastry into four 6-inch squares. Spread scant 2 tablespoons almond paste mixture over center 4 inches of each square. Place ¼ cup plum mixture atop center of almond paste mixture on each. Brush 2 sides of pastry edges with glaze. Fold pastry over filling, forming triangle and pressing edges to adhere. Press edges with fork to seal. Transfer turnovers to baking sheet. Repeat procedure with remaining pastry sheet, almond paste mixture and plum mixture.

Cut small hole and a few slits in top of each turnover to allow steam to escape. Brush turnovers with glaze. Sprinkle with 1 tablespoon sugar. Freeze 20 minutes. *(Can be prepared 1 week ahead. Cover and keep frozen. Thaw 6 hours in refrigerator.)*

Position 1 rack in center and 1 rack in top third of oven; preheat to 375°F. Bake turnovers until golden, switching top and bottom baking sheets halfway through baking, about 30 minutes. Cool on baking sheets. Serve at room temperature.

8 SERVINGS

White Chocolate Tartlets with Strawberry Coulis

◆ ◆ ◆

CRUSTS

8   ounces purchased almond biscotti

1   cup whole almonds, toasted (about 5½ ounces)

½   cup (1 stick) unsalted butter, melted

FILLING

1¼   cups whipping cream

8   ounces white chocolate (such as Lindt or Baker's), chopped

12   ounces cream cheese, room temperature

3   tablespoons sugar

5   teaspoons vanilla extract

COULIS

2   cups quartered hulled strawberries (about 12 ounces)

¼   cup water

3   tablespoons sugar

2   teaspoons fresh lemon juice

Strawberries, water, sugar and lemon juice are made into a delicious coulis, a French term that refers to a thick puree or sauce. The crust for the tartlets is simply ground biscotti and almonds mixed with butter.

◆ ◆ ◆

FOR CRUSTS: Preheat oven to 350°F. Grind biscotti and almonds in processor until finely ground. Add butter and process until well blended. Divide mixture equally among eight 4½-inch-diameter tartlet pans with removable bottoms (about ⅓ cup mixture for each). Press mixture onto bottoms and up sides of pans. Bake until crusts are golden brown, about 15 minutes. Transfer pans to racks; cool.

FOR FILLING: Bring ½ cup whipping cream to boil in heavy medium saucepan. Remove from heat. Add chopped white chocolate and stir until melted and smooth. Cool mixture to room temperature. Using electric mixer, beat cream cheese in large bowl until smooth. Gradually add white chocolate mixture and beat until well blended. Beat remaining ¾ cup whipping cream, sugar and vanilla in medium bowl until medium-firm peaks form. Fold into cream cheese mixture in 2 additions. Divide filling among prepared tartlet crusts (about ½ cup for each). Chill at least 2 hours.

FOR COULIS: Combine berries, water, sugar and juice in blender. Puree until smooth. Chill until cold, at least 2 hours. *(Tartlets and coulis can be made 1 day ahead. Keep chilled.)*

Remove tartlets from pans. Place 1 tartlet on each of 8 plates. Spoon strawberry coulis alongside and serve.

MAKES 8

Desserts
175

Three-Citrus Meringue Tart

◆ ◆ ◆

While the meringue topping of this pretty tart is light, the lemon, orange and lime custard filling has appealing richness. Plus, the tart is relatively low in fat and calories.

◆ ◆ ◆

CRUST

Nonstick vegetable oil spray
½ cup all purpose flour
2 tablespoons sugar
2 tablespoons (¼ stick) unsalted butter, melted

FILLING

¼ cup sugar
1½ tablespoons all purpose flour
½ teaspoon baking powder
¼ teaspoon salt
3 large egg whites
1 large egg
2 tablespoons fresh lemon juice
2 tablespoons fresh orange juice
2 tablespoons fresh lime juice
¾ teaspoon grated lemon peel
¾ teaspoon grated orange peel
¾ teaspoon grated lime peel

TOPPING

2 large egg whites
⅛ teaspoon cream of tartar
2 tablespoons sugar
¼ teaspoon grated lemon peel
¼ teaspoon grated orange peel
¼ teaspoon grated lime peel

FOR CRUST: Preheat oven to 350°F. Spray 8 x 8 x 2-inch metal baking pan with nonstick vegetable oil spray. Mix flour and sugar in large bowl. Add melted butter and stir with fork until mixture forms coarse crumbs (mixture will be dry). Using fingers, press crumbs over bottom of prepared baking pan. Bake until crust is set and light golden, about 20 minutes. Cool crust completely on wire rack. Maintain oven temperature.

FOR FILLING: Mix first 4 ingredients in small bowl. Whisk egg whites, egg, juices and peels in medium bowl. Add flour mixture; whisk until smooth. Pour filling over crust.

Bake tart until filling is set, about 18 minutes. Cool completely on rack. *(Can be made 1 day ahead. Cover and chill.)*

FOR TOPPING: Preheat oven to 350°F. Beat egg whites and cream of tartar in clean large bowl until soft peaks form. Add sugar 1 tablespoon at a time and beat until stiff peaks form. Spoon meringue over filling, covering completely. Sprinkle peels atop meringue. Bake until meringue tips begin to brown, about 10 minutes. Transfer to rack. Cool completely. Cut into 6 pieces.

6 SERVINGS

Lemon Tart Brûlée

◆ ◆ ◆

CRUST

1⅓ cups all purpose flour

2 tablespoons sugar

2 teaspoons grated lemon peel

⅛ teaspoon salt

½ cup (1 stick) chilled unsalted butter, cut into ½-inch pieces

2 tablespoons (about) cold water

FILLING

3 large eggs

½ cup plus 1 tablespoon sugar

⅓ cup whipping cream

⅓ cup fresh lemon juice

1 tablespoon grated lemon peel
   Pinch of salt

FOR CRUST: Blend flour, sugar, grated lemon peel and salt in processor. Add butter; cut in using on/off turns until mixture resembles coarse meal. Mix in enough water to form dough. Turn dough out onto work surface. Gather dough into ball and flatten into disk. Wrap in plastic; refrigerate 1 hour.

Preheat oven to 400°F. Roll out dough on floured surface to 13-inch round. Transfer dough to 9-inch-diameter tart pan with removable bottom. Trim overhang to ½ inch. Fold overhang under, pressing to form double-thick sides. Freeze crust 15 minutes.

Bake crust until pale golden brown, about 20 minutes. Cool.

FOR FILLING: Whisk eggs, ½ cup sugar, cream, lemon juice, peel and salt in bowl to blend. Pour filling into crust (filling will not fill crust). Bake until set, about 25 minutes. Cool completely.

Preheat broiler. Sprinkle remaining 1 tablespoon sugar over tart. Cover sides of crust with foil to protect from heat. Broil tart until sugar caramelizes in spots, watching closely, about 3 minutes. Serve tart warm or at room temperature.

8 SERVINGS

◆ ◆ ◆

This superb lemon tart has a caramelized top—just like the one on a crème brûlée. As added embellishment, it can be served with a custard sauce and sliced strawberries.

Pear Tart with Butterscotch Sauce

◆ ◆ ◆

◆ ◆ ◆

This recipe makes two large tarts, which will serve approximately 20 people. That, combined with the fact that the tarts can be prepared ahead, makes this an ideal "entertaining" recipe. Of course, the ingredients can be halved if your gathering is smaller.

◆ ◆ ◆

PEARS

6	cups water
⅔	cup sugar
2	vanilla beans, split lengthwise
8	medium Anjou pears (about 3¼ pounds total)

CRUST

2½	cups all purpose flour
¾	cup cake flour
½	cup sugar
1	cup (2 sticks) chilled unsalted butter, cut into ½-inch pieces
6	tablespoons chilled solid vegetable shortening, cut into ½-inch pieces
4	tablespoons (about) ice water

FILLING

1½	cups slivered almonds, toasted
¾	cup (1½ sticks) unsalted butter, cut into pieces, room temperature
¾	cup sugar
4	large eggs
2	large egg whites
2	teaspoons vanilla extract

Butterscotch Sauce (see recipe opposite)

FOR PEARS: Combine 6 cups water and sugar in heavy large wide saucepan. Scrape in seeds from vanilla beans; add beans. Bring to simmer, stirring until sugar dissolves. Peel, halve and core pears. Add pears to vanilla syrup and simmer until tender, about 10 minutes. Cool pears in syrup. *(Can be prepared 1 day ahead. Cover pears in syrup and refrigerate overnight.)*

FOR CRUST: Blend both flours and sugar in processor. Add butter and shortening; cut in using on/off turns until mixture resembles coarse meal. Blend in water by tablespoonfuls until dough begins to clump together. Gather into ball; divide in half. Flatten each half into disk. Wrap each in plastic and chill 1 hour.

Preheat oven to 375°F. Roll out 1 dough disk between sheets of plastic to 13-inch round. Peel off top sheet. Using bottom sheet as aid, invert dough into 11-inch-diameter tart pan with removable bottom. Peel off plastic. Press dough into bottom and up sides of pan. Repeat with second disk and second pan. Freeze crusts 15 minutes.

Line crusts with foil. Fill with dried beans or pie weights. Bake until crusts are set, about 10 minutes. Remove foil and beans. Bake crusts until golden, about 20 minutes. Transfer to rack; cool.

FOR FILLING: Preheat oven to 350°F. Finely grind almonds in processor. Add butter and sugar; blend well. Add eggs, egg whites and vanilla and blend well.

Using slotted spoon, remove pears from syrup (reserve syrup for another use). Cut lengthwise into ¼-inch-thick slices.

Pour half of filling into each crust. Fan half of pear slices atop filling in each crust, overlapping slices slightly. Bake until tops brown and filling is set, about 25 minutes. Cool tarts in pans on racks. *(Can be made 8 hours ahead. Cover; let stand at room temperature.)*

Remove pan sides. Drizzle ¼ cup Butterscotch Sauce over each tart. Pass remaining sauce separately.

MAKES TWO 11-INCH TARTS

Butterscotch Sauce

3	cups sugar
⅔	cup water
1½	cups whipping cream
½	cup (1 stick) unsalted butter, cut into pieces
1	teaspoon vanilla extract

Stir sugar and water in heavy large saucepan over medium-low heat until sugar dissolves. Increase heat; boil without stirring until syrup turns deep amber, brushing down pan sides with pastry brush dipped into water and swirling pan occasionally. Remove from heat. Add cream and butter (mixture will bubble vigorously). Return to heat; stir until sauce is smooth. Cool. Add vanilla. *(Can be prepared 2 days ahead. Cover; chill. Stir over medium heat just until liquid, but not hot, before using.)*

MAKES ABOUT 3 CUPS

◆ FRUIT DESSERTS ◆

Brown Sugar Pineapple Brûlée

◆ ◆ ◆

1   3-pound pineapple

1   tablespoon butter
⅓   cup (packed) golden brown sugar
1   tablespoon water
½   teaspoon ground cinnamon
2   tablespoons dark rum

Line baking sheet with foil. Using large sharp knife, quarter pineapple lengthwise through leafy top. Core each wedge. Cut pineapple flesh from peel of each wedge, keeping flesh in 1 piece. Set aside. Transfer pineapple shells to baking sheet. Cover pineapple leaves with foil to protect from heat.

Preheat broiler. Melt butter in heavy large skillet over medium heat. Add sugar, water and cinnamon. Bring to boil, stirring until sugar dissolves. Remove from heat. Add rum to sauce; ignite with match. *(Pineapple and sauce can be prepared 1 day ahead. Cover pineapple and sauce separately. Bring sauce to simmer before continuing.)* Add pineapple wedges to skillet. Cook until heated through, turning to coat, about 4 minutes. Return pineapple to shells. Boil sauce until thick, about 2 minutes.

Cut each pineapple wedge crosswise into ½-inch-thick slices, keeping shells intact. Spoon sauce over pineapple. Broil until sauce bubbles and browns slightly, about 3 minutes. Transfer to plates.

4 SERVINGS

Pear and Raspberry Cobbler with Buttermilk Biscuits

◆ ◆ ◆

FILLING
3   pounds firm but ripe Anjou pears, peeled, cored, cut in ¾-inch pieces
¼   cup sugar
2   tablespoons all purpose flour
1   teaspoon vanilla extract
1   cup frozen raspberries (unthawed)

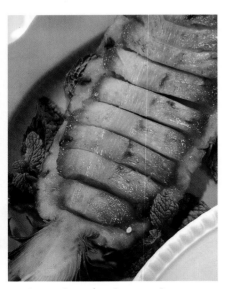

A cored pineapple is used to serve this low-calorie, low-fat dessert (wedges of the fruit topped with a cinnamon-rum sauce and broiled until golden brown), so be sure to select one with bright leaves.

◆ ◆ ◆

BISCUITS

1½ cups all purpose flour

2 tablespoons sugar

1½ teaspoons baking powder

¾ teaspoon baking soda

¼ teaspoon salt

5 tablespoons chilled unsalted butter, cut into pieces

½ cup buttermilk

½ cup whipping cream

½ teaspoon vanilla extract

Additional sugar
Vanilla ice cream

FOR FILLING: Preheat oven to 375°F. Combine pears, sugar, flour and vanilla in large bowl. Toss to coat. Transfer half of pear mixture to 8 x 8 x 2-inch glass baking dish. Sprinkle berries atop pears. Top with remaining pear mixture. Cover with foil; bake pear mixture until bubbling, about 35 minutes.

MEANWHILE, PREPARE BISCUITS: Combine first 5 ingredients in large bowl. Add butter; rub in with fingertips until mixture resembles coarse meal. Whisk buttermilk, cream and vanilla in medium bowl to blend. Add to flour mixture; stir until soft sticky dough forms.

Drop large spoonfuls of dough onto hot pear mixture. Sprinkle with sugar. Bake uncovered until biscuits are golden, about 25 minutes. Serve with vanilla ice cream.

6 SERVINGS

Juicy Anjou pears and frozen raspberries make up the filling, while tender buttermilk biscuits top the cobbler. Vanilla ice cream rounds out this delicious homespun dessert.

Marsala Baked Apples

◆ ◆ ◆

2	cups apple cider
1	cup dry Marsala
6	medium Golden Delicious apples
8	tablespoons (packed) golden brown sugar
6	tablespoons golden raisins
¼	teaspoon ground nutmeg
3	tablespoons unsalted butter
	Vanilla ice cream
6	almond biscotti

Boil apple cider and Marsala in heavy medium saucepan until reduced to 1 cup, about 20 minutes. *(Syrup can be made 1 day ahead. Cover and refrigerate.)*

Preheat oven to 350°F. Peel top quarter of each apple. Core apples without cutting through bottom. Place in 8 x 8 x 2-inch glass baking dish. Spoon 1 tablespoon golden brown sugar, then 1 tablespoon golden raisins into each apple.

Stir 2 tablespoons golden brown sugar into syrup. Pour syrup over and around apples. Sprinkle ground nutmeg over. Place ½ tablespoon butter atop center of each apple.

Bake apples until butter melts, about 5 minutes. Cover dish with foil; bake 30 minutes. Uncover and bake until apples are tender, basting frequently with juices, about 25 minutes longer.

Serve apples hot or warm in bowls with ice cream and biscotti.

6 SERVINGS

◆ ◆ ◆

Filled with raisins and brown sugar and baked in Marsala and cider, these apples make a warming ending to a cool-weather meal. Accompany them with vanilla ice cream and purchased biscotti.

◆ ◆ ◆

Apricot-Cherry Shortcakes

◆ ◆ ◆

BISCUITS

Nonstick vegetable oil spray

½	cup low-fat buttermilk
1½	teaspoons grated orange peel
½	teaspoon ground nutmeg
1¼	cups all purpose flour

3	tablespoons sugar
½	teaspoon baking powder
½	teaspoon baking soda
⅛	teaspoon salt
1	tablespoon chilled vegetable shortening, cut into small pieces
1	tablespoon chilled unsalted butter, cut into small pieces

FRUIT

1	tablespoon water
2	teaspoons cornstarch
1	11½-ounce can apricot nectar
3	tablespoons sugar
1	teaspoon fresh lemon juice
1	pound apricots, quartered, pitted
1	pound Bing cherries, halved, pitted
½	teaspoon vanilla extract

Here's a light version (weighing in at under 300 calories and 6 grams of fat per serving) of an American classic, best made when apricots and cherries are at their ripest.

◆ ◆ ◆

FOR BISCUITS: Preheat oven to 425°F. Lightly spray heavy baking sheet with vegetable oil spray.

Mix buttermilk, orange peel and nutmeg in small bowl. Mix flour, sugar, baking powder, baking soda and salt in large bowl. Add shortening and butter to flour mixture and rub in with fingertips until mixture resembles coarse meal. Add buttermilk mixture and stir until soft dough forms. Turn dough out onto lightly floured surface and gently knead until smooth, about 4 to 5 turns. Pat biscuit dough into 6 x 4-inch rectangle. Cut dough into 6 equal squares.

Transfer biscuits to prepared baking sheet. Bake until puffed and golden, about 12 minutes. Transfer to rack and cool slightly. *(Can be made 4 hours ahead. Cool completely. Before serving, cover with foil and rewarm in 350°F oven 5 minutes.)*

FOR FRUIT: Mix water and cornstarch in small bowl to blend. Bring apricot nectar, sugar and lemon juice to boil in heavy medium saucepan. Whisk in cornstarch mixture. Bring to boil, stirring constantly. Mix in apricots, Bing cherries and vanilla extract. Reduce heat to medium and stir until sauce thickens slightly and fruit mixture is warmed through, about 1 minute.

Cut warm biscuits horizontally in half. Place 1 bottom onto each of 6 plates. Spoon half of fruit mixture over, dividing equally. Place tops over fruit. Spoon remaining fruit mixture over each.

6 SERVINGS

Pears Poached in Red Wine, Cardamom and Orange

◆ ◆ ◆

1   750-ml bottle dry red wine
2¼ cups sugar
2   cups water
½   cup orange juice
2   teaspoons grated orange peel
1   teaspoon ground cardamom
1   cinnamon stick
4   firm but ripe pears, peeled, stems left intact

1   pint vanilla ice cream
1   plain or almond biscotti, crumbled
     Orange peel strips (optional)

A cardamom- and orange-scented syrup is spooned over warm pears and scoops of vanilla ice cream in this lovely dessert. Refrigerate leftover poaching syrup to serve over scoops of ice cream at another meal.

◆ ◆ ◆

Combine first 7 ingredients in heavy large saucepan. Stir over medium heat until sugar dissolves and mixture comes to simmer. Add pears and return mixture to simmer. Reduce heat and simmer slowly until pears are tender when pierced with knife, about 25 minutes. Transfer pears to plate. Boil liquid in saucepan until reduced to 3 cups, about 20 minutes. *(Can be made 1 day ahead. Cover and chill pears in poaching liquid. Before serving, rewarm over medium-low heat until pears are heated through.)*

Arrange 1 warm pear and 1 scoop of ice cream on each of 4 plates. Drizzle some poaching liquid over. Sprinkle with biscotti crumbs. Garnish with orange peel strips, if desired, and serve.

4 SERVINGS

Oranges in Cinnamon Syrup

◆ ◆ ◆

½   cup dry white wine
½   cup water
¼   cup sugar
1   cinnamon stick, broken in half

3   large navel oranges, peel and white pith removed, ends trimmed, each cut into 4 rounds

Combine white wine, water, sugar and cinnamon stick in small saucepan. Bring wine mixture to boil. Reduce heat; cover and simmer 8 minutes. Remove syrup from heat.

Arrange orange rounds in single layer in wide shallow bowl. Pour hot syrup and cinnamon stick over oranges. Refrigerate at least 3 hours. *(Can be made 1 day ahead. Cover and keep chilled.)*

4 SERVINGS

Strawberries and Grapes with Mint and Vanilla

◆ ◆ ◆

2	12- to 16-ounce baskets strawberries, hulled, quartered
2	cups seedless green grapes
¼	cup sugar
2	teaspoons finely chopped fresh mint
¼	teaspoon vanilla extract

Combine all ingredients in large bowl; toss to coat fruit. Cover; chill at least 1 hour and up to 4 hours. Spoon fruit into bowls.

4 SERVINGS

Fresh Fruit Cocktail with Sorbet

◆ ◆ ◆

2	cups diced peeled pineapple
2	cups diced peeled pitted mango
2	cups diced peeled seeded papaya
1	12-ounce basket strawberries, hulled, quartered
1½	cups peach-passion fruit nectar
1¼	cups diced peeled kiwi
3	tablespoons thinly sliced fresh mint
2½	cups lime or mango sorbet

Combine all ingredients except sorbet in large bowl. Cover and chill for 15 minutes or up to 4 hours. Spoon fruit into 10 Martini glasses. Top with scoop of sorbet and serve.

10 SERVINGS

Hazelnut Dome Cake

◆ ◆ ◆

This impressive-looking dessert is achieved by lining a large bowl with thin slices of cake. A layer of chocolate ganache is spread over the cake, which is filled with hazelnut cream. The gorgeous result is garnished with mixed raspberries and blackberries.

CAKE

Nonstick vegetable oil spray
2⅔ cups blanched slivered almonds (about 11 ounces), toasted
1¾ cups hazelnuts (about 7 ounces), toasted
2 cups sugar
½ cup cake flour
9 large egg whites

CHOCOLATE GANACHE

10 ounces bittersweet (not unsweetened) or semisweet chocolate, chopped
2 cups whipping cream

HAZELNUT CREAM

2 cups chilled whipping cream
¼ cup sugar
¼ cup plus 3 tablespoons amaretto or other almond liqueur
½ cup hazelnuts, toasted, husked, chopped (about 2 ounces)
⅓ cup finely chopped semisweet chocolate (about 2 ounces)

Unsweetened cocoa powder
Powdered sugar
Fresh raspberries and blackberries

FOR CAKE: Preheat oven to 350°F. Spray 15 x 10 x 1-inch baking sheet with nonstick spray. Line with parchment paper. Butter parchment. Combine nuts, sugar and flour in processor. Process until nuts are finely ground. Beat egg whites in large bowl until stiff peaks form. Fold nut mixture into whites in 3 additions (whites will deflate). Spread on prepared baking sheet. Bake until cake starts to pull away from sides of sheet and is light golden on top, about 35 minutes (cake will be slightly moist). Cool cake 10 minutes.

Line another large baking sheet with parchment paper. Invert cake onto parchment. Cool cake completely.

FOR CHOCOLATE GANACHE: Place chopped chocolate in large bowl. Bring cream to simmer in heavy medium saucepan. Pour over

chocolate and whisk until smooth. Chill ganache until firm enough to spread, at least 6 hours or overnight. *(Cake and chocolate ganache can be made 1 day ahead. Cover cake tightly with plastic wrap; leave at room temperature. Keep ganache refrigerated. Let stand at room temperature until spreadable.)*

FOR HAZELNUT CREAM: Beat cream in large bowl until soft peaks form. Gradually add sugar and ¼ cup amaretto, beating until stiff peaks form. Fold in chopped hazelnuts and chocolate.

Line 2-quart bowl with plastic wrap, overlapping sides by 2 inches. Cut cake lengthwise into ⅓-inch-wide slices. Line bowl with cake, placing slices cut side down and tightly side by side in single layer, trimming to fit and completely covering bowl (if cake slices break, piece together to fit). Brush cake with 1½ tablespoons amaretto. Spread chocolate ganache over cake, covering completely. Spoon hazelnut cream into center; smooth top. Cover filling with cake, placing slices side by side, fitting tightly together and trimming to fit. Brush with 1½ tablespoons amaretto. Cover and refrigerate at least 4 hours and up to 3 days.

Uncover cake. Invert onto platter. Remove plastic. Sift cocoa powder and powdered sugar over. Serve with berries.

12 TO 14 SERVINGS

Lemon Cheesecake with Hazelnut Crust

◆ ◆ ◆

CRUST

¾ cup hazelnuts, toasted

¾ cup graham cracker crumbs

3 tablespoons powdered sugar

5 tablespoons unsalted butter, melted

FILLING

3 8-ounce packages cream cheese, room temperature

1 cup sugar

3 large eggs

¼ cup fresh lemon juice

1 tablespoon grated lemon peel

Lemon slices (optional)

Fresh mint sprigs (optional)

FOR CRUST: Position rack in center of oven and preheat to 350°F. Finely grind nuts, cracker crumbs and sugar in processor. Add butter; blend using on/off turns until crumbs are moist. Press crumbs onto bottom and ½ inch up sides of 9-inch-diameter spring-form pan with 2¾-inch-high sides. Chill while making filling.

FOR FILLING: Using electric mixer, beat cream cheese in large bowl until fluffy. Slowly add sugar; beat until smooth. Add eggs 1 at a time, beating 30 seconds after each. Mix in lemon juice and peel.

Pour filling into crust. Bake cake until outer 2-inch portion of top is set and center looks slightly glossy and is barely set, about 45 minutes. Transfer cheesecake to rack; cool to room temperature. Cover cheesecake and refrigerate overnight.

Run knife around sides of pan to loosen. Release pan sides. Place cake on plate. Top with lemon and mint, if desired.

8 TO 10 SERVINGS

Applesauce Coffee Cake with Crumb Topping

◆ ◆ ◆

TOPPING

¼   cup all purpose flour
¼   cup (packed) golden brown sugar
3   tablespoons unsalted butter, room temperature
½   teaspoon ground cinnamon

CAKE

     Nonstick vegetable oil spray
1½ cups all purpose flour
¼   cup (packed) golden brown sugar
2   teaspoons baking powder
½   teaspoon baking soda
½   teaspoon salt
½   cup unsweetened applesauce
⅓   cup low-fat buttermilk
2   tablespoons vegetable oil
1   large egg yolk
1   teaspoon vanilla extract
½   teaspoon (packed) grated lemon peel
2   large egg whites

FOR TOPPING: Preheat oven to 350°F. Combine flour, brown sugar, butter and cinnamon in small bowl. Mash with fork until blended and coarse crumbs form. Set aside.

FOR CAKE: Spray 9-inch-diameter cake pan with 1½-inch-high sides with vegetable oil spray. Sift flour, sugar, baking powder, baking soda and salt into large bowl. Whisk applesauce, buttermilk, oil, egg yolk, vanilla and lemon peel in medium bowl to blend. Add to dry ingredients and stir just until moistened (batter will be thick). Beat egg whites in another large bowl until stiff peaks form. Whisk half of whites into batter. Fold in remaining whites.

Transfer batter to prepared pan. Sprinkle topping over batter. Bake cake until tester inserted into center comes out clean, about 30 minutes. Transfer to rack; cool in pan. Cut into 10 wedges.

10 SERVINGS

Cherry Upside-Down Cake

◆ ◆ ◆

TOPPING
¼ cup (½ stick) unsalted butter
¾ cup (packed) golden brown sugar
14 ounces cherries, halved, pitted

CAKE
1½ cups all purpose flour
2 teaspoons baking powder
¼ teaspoon salt
1 cup sugar
½ cup (1 stick) unsalted butter, room temperature
2 large eggs, separated
1½ teaspoons vanilla extract
½ cup milk (do not use low-fat or nonfat)

¼ teaspoon cream of tartar

1 cup chilled whipping cream
1½ tablespoons powdered sugar

FOR TOPPING: Preheat oven to 350°F. Butter sides of 9-inch-diameter cake pan with 2-inch-high sides. Melt ¼ cup butter in same pan set over low heat. Add brown sugar; whisk until well blended, about 2 minutes. Remove from heat. Spread over bottom of pan. Arrange cherries, cut side down, in single layer in bottom of pan.

FOR CAKE: Mix flour, baking powder and salt in medium bowl. Using electric mixer, beat 1 cup sugar and butter in large bowl until creamy. Mix in yolks 1 at a time, beating well after each. Beat in 1 teaspoon vanilla. Mix in dry ingredients alternately with milk.

Using clean dry beaters, beat egg whites and cream of tartar in another large bowl until stiff but not dry. Stir ¼ of whites into cake batter to lighten. Using rubber spatula, gently fold remaining whites into batter. Spoon batter atop cherries in pan. Bake cake until deep golden on top and tester inserted into center comes out clean, about 55 minutes. Cool cake in pan on rack 15 minutes.

Whip cream, sugar and ½ teaspoon vanilla to soft peaks.

Run small knife around edges of pan to loosen cake. Place platter over cake and invert onto platter. Let stand 5 minutes. Remove pan. Serve cake warm or at room temperature with whipped cream.

8 SERVINGS

◆ ◆ ◆

Fresh cherries take center stage in this tasty version of an old favorite. Make both the cake and the whipped cream topping up to six hours ahead, leaving the cake at room temperature (covered) and refrigerating the cream.

◆ ◆ ◆

Chocolate-Espresso Cheesecake

◆ ◆ ◆

1¼ cups chocolate wafer crumbs (about 24 cookies)
2½ tablespoons unsalted butter, melted

3 tablespoons brandy
2 tablespoons instant espresso powder
6 ounces bittersweet (not unsweetened) or semisweet chocolate, finely chopped

4 8-ounce packages cream cheese, room temperature
1¼ cups sugar
½ cup whipping cream
⅓ cup sour cream
1 tablespoon vanilla extract
3 large eggs, room temperature

Chocolate curls (optional)

Coffee and bittersweet chocolate star in this luscious layered cheesecake. Be sure to start preparing it a day ahead to allow the cake to set up in the refrigerator overnight.

Preheat oven to 350°F. Stir chocolate wafer crumbs and butter in medium bowl until crumbs are moist. Press mixture onto bottom (not sides) of 9-inch-diameter springform pan with 2¾-inch-high sides. Bake crust until just firm to touch, approximately 7 minutes. Cool crust. Maintain oven temperature.

Stir brandy and espresso powder in small bowl until espresso dissolves. Stir chocolate in top of double boiler over simmering water until smooth. Remove from over water. Cool to lukewarm.

Using electric mixer, beat cream cheese, sugar, whipping cream, sour cream and vanilla in large bowl until smooth. Beat in eggs 1 at a time. Transfer half of batter to medium bowl. Add melted chocolate to batter in medium bowl; stir until well blended. Stir espresso mixture into batter in large bowl.

Pour chocolate batter onto prepared crust. Bake until chocolate layer just begins to set, about 20 minutes.

Carefully spoon espresso batter over chocolate layer. Bake cake until sides puff slightly and center is softly set but still appears moist, about 45 minutes. Transfer cheesecake to rack; cool. Cover pan and refrigerate cheesecake overnight.

Cut around pan sides to loosen cake; release pan sides. Garnish top of cake with chocolate curls, if desired.

10 SERVINGS

Chocolate-Almond Soufflé Torte

◆ ◆ ◆

1	cup (about 5 ounces) whole almonds, toasted, cooled
4	tablespoons plus ⅓ cup sugar
2	tablespoons vegetable oil
¾	cup (1½ sticks) unsalted butter
½	cup whipping cream
1	pound bittersweet (not unsweetened) or semisweet chocolate, finely chopped
6	large eggs, separated, room temperature
1	cup chilled whipping cream
2	tablespoons amaretto or 1 teaspoon almond extract
	Powdered sugar
½	cup almond slices, toasted

Position rack in center of oven and preheat to 350°F. Butter and flour 9-inch-diameter springform pan with 2¾-inch-high sides. Shake out excess flour. Line bottom of pan with parchment paper; butter parchment paper. Set aside.

Combine ½ cup whole almonds and 2 tablespoons sugar in processor. Using on/off turns, grind nuts finely. Transfer almond mixture to large bowl. Combine remaining ½ cup whole almonds and vegetable oil in processor. Process until mixture is thick and pasty (consistency will be similar to that of peanut butter), scraping processor bowl frequently, about 3 minutes.

Stir butter and ½ cup whipping cream in heavy large saucepan over medium heat until butter melts and mixture simmers. Remove from heat. Add chocolate and whisk until smooth. Stir in both almond mixtures. Cool chocolate mixture slightly.

Using electric mixer, beat egg whites in large bowl until soft peaks form. Gradually add ⅓ cup sugar and beat until stiff peaks form. Beat egg yolks in another large bowl until very pale and thick, about 5 minutes. Gradually beat chocolate mixture into egg yolks. Fold in egg whites in 3 additions.

Pour batter into prepared pan. Bake cake until sides crack and puff and tester inserted into center comes out with moist batter attached, about 35 minutes. Transfer cake to rack. Cool cake to room temperature, about 2 hours (center will fall slightly as cake cools). *(Can be prepared 4 days ahead. Cover and refrigerate.)*

◆ ◆ ◆

Offer this dessert (pictured on page 168) at room temperature if you like a creamy texture similar to that of a soufflé, or serve the cake cold if you prefer a dense, fudgy texture.

◆ ◆ ◆

Beat chilled cream, amaretto and remaining 2 tablespoons sugar in large bowl until soft peaks form.

Run small sharp knife around pan sides to loosen cake. Release pan sides. Dust cake with powdered sugar. Sprinkle toasted almond slices around top edge of cake. Serve chilled or at room temperature with sweetened whipped cream.

12 TO 14 SERVINGS

Chocolate Mint Layer Cake with Mint Cream Cheese Frosting

◆ ◆ ◆

2¼ cups sugar

2 cups all purpose flour

¾ cup unsweetened cocoa powder

1 teaspoon baking soda

½ teaspoon salt

1½ cups milk (do not use low-fat or nonfat), hot

1 cup (2 sticks) unsalted butter, melted, hot

2 large eggs

1½ teaspoons peppermint extract

3 8-ounce packages cream cheese, room temperature

5 cups powdered sugar

½ cup (1 stick) unsalted butter, room temperature

Preheat oven to 350°F. Line 15½ x 10½ x 1-inch baking sheet with waxed paper. Mix first 5 ingredients in large bowl. Whisk in milk and melted butter, then eggs and ¾ teaspoon peppermint extract. Spread batter evenly in pan.

Bake until tester inserted into center of cake comes out clean, about 25 minutes. Cool cake in pan on rack.

Using electric mixer, beat cream cheese, powdered sugar, ½ cup butter and ¾ teaspoon peppermint extract in large bowl to blend.

Run small sharp knife around sides of pan to loosen cake. Turn cake out onto work surface. Peel off paper. Cut cake crosswise in half. Using spatula, place 1 cake half on platter and spread with 2 cups cream cheese frosting. Top with remaining cake half. Spread remaining frosting over top and sides of cake.

10 TO 12 SERVINGS

CURDS OF ALL KINDS

In eighteenth-century England, tart and tangy lemon curd was used as a preserve and spread on toast, cakes and pastries. Later, in Victorian times, it was used in little tarts, called lemon cheese cakes (the English often refer to lemon curd as lemon cheese or lemon butter). Lemon curd made the transition into American cooking by way of a few colonists, who brought the recipe with them to the New World. Only recently, though, has it become relatively commonplace, with many a refrigerator sporting a jar of the stuff right alongside the ketchup and jam.

Most of the curd that is available in stores is lemon flavored, but the surprisingly simple recipe for the homemade kind lends itself to a variety of flavorings, from lime, orange and berry to passion fruit, apple and apricot. The extracted juice is mixed with egg yolks, sugar, a little salt and butter, then heated until thickened. The resulting curd may be kept in a jar in the refrigerator for two weeks.

◆ ◆ ◆

Lemon Curd Mousse with Toasted Coconut and Blueberries

◆ ◆ ◆

2	teaspoons water
½	teaspoon unflavored gelatin
1	cup sugar
½	cup fresh lemon juice
6	large egg yolks
2	tablespoons grated lemon peel
¾	cup (1½ sticks) unsalted butter, cut into small pieces
1	cup sweetened flaked coconut
¼	cup (packed) golden brown sugar
1½	cups chilled whipping cream
2	6-ounce baskets fresh blueberries

Place 2 teaspoons water in small bowl; sprinkle gelatin over. Let stand 10 minutes. Whisk sugar, lemon juice, yolks and lemon peel in heavy medium saucepan to blend. Add butter; stir constantly over medium heat until mixture thickens and just begins to bubble at edges, about 9 minutes. Remove from heat. Add gelatin mixture; stir to dissolve. Transfer lemon curd to medium bowl. Press plastic wrap directly onto surface. Refrigerate until cold. *(Can be prepared 3 days ahead. Keep refrigerated.)*

Preheat oven to 350°F. Spread coconut on baking sheet. Sprinkle brown sugar over. Bake until coconut is golden, stirring occasionally, about 10 minutes. Cool.

Beat cream in medium bowl until stiff peaks form. Fold 1 cup whipped cream into lemon curd.

Layer 3 tablespoons berries, 3 tablespoons mousse, 1 tablespoon coconut mixture and 3 tablespoons whipped cream in each of 8 stemmed 10- to 12-ounce glasses. Repeat layering. Top each with 2 tablespoons berries, dollop of cream, some coconut mixture and more berries. *(Can be made 6 hours ahead. Cover; chill.)*

8 SERVINGS

Bread Pudding with Currants

◆ ◆ ◆

5   cups half and half
1   tablespoon plus 1 teaspoon minced orange peel
1½   teaspoons aniseed
1   vanilla bean, cut in half lengthwise

4   large eggs
2   large egg yolks
¾   cup plus 2 tablespoons sugar

1   10-ounce sourdough baguette, crust trimmed, cut into ¾-inch cubes
3   tablespoons dried currants

Mix half and half, 1 tablespoon orange peel and aniseed in heavy large saucepan. Scrape in seeds from vanilla bean; add bean. Bring to simmer. Remove from heat. Cover; let stand 30 minutes.

Whisk eggs and yolks in large bowl to blend. Gradually whisk in warm half and half mixture. Strain custard into bowl. Add sugar and 1 teaspoon orange peel to custard. Stir until sugar dissolves.

Place bread in 8 x 8 x 2-inch glass baking dish. Sprinkle currants over. Pour custard over. Cover with plastic. Chill until bread absorbs some custard, occasionally pressing on bread, 1 hour.

Preheat oven to 350°F. Remove plastic from pudding. Bake until custard is set and bread starts to brown, about 1 hour. Let stand at least 15 minutes. Serve bread pudding hot or warm.

6 SERVINGS

Mango Flans

◆ ◆ ◆

1½   cups plus ⅓ cup sugar
¾   cup hot water
2   tablespoons light corn syrup

2   1-pound ripe mangoes, peeled, pitted, pureed
1   tablespoon plus 1 teaspoon fresh lime juice
½   teaspoon ground ginger
¾   cup plus 2 tablespoons half and half
5   large eggs

Preheat oven to 350°F. Combine 1½ cups sugar, ¾ cup hot water and corn syrup in heavy medium saucepan. Stir over medium-low

Many varieties of mango are grown in most tropical countries, including much of Central and South America and the Caribbean. This dessert makes delicious use of the popular fruit. Begin preparing these individual flans at least six hours ahead.

◆ ◆ ◆

heat until sugar dissolves. Increase heat and boil without stirring until syrup is deep amber, occasionally brushing down sides of pan with wet pastry brush and swirling pan, about 6 minutes. Pour caramel syrup into eight 6-ounce custard cups, dividing equally.

Whisk mango puree, lime juice, ginger and ⅓ cup sugar in heavy medium saucepan over medium-high heat until mixture thickens and large bubbles break surface, about 5 minutes. Cool slightly, stirring occasionally. Whisk half and half and eggs in large bowl to blend. Stir in mango mixture. Strain custard.

Pour custard over caramel in custard cups, dividing equally. Place custard cups in large roasting pan. Pour enough hot water into pan to come halfway up sides of cups. Cover pan with foil.

Bake flans until just set in center, about 35 minutes. Turn off heat. Leave flans covered in oven 30 minutes longer. Remove from roasting pan. Cover and refrigerate at least 6 hours or overnight.

Run small sharp knife around sides of 1 custard cup. Place plate atop cup. Invert flan onto plate, letting caramel run over top of flan. Remove custard cup. Repeat with remaining flans and serve.

8 SERVINGS

New-Style Old-fashioned Chocolate Pudding

◆ ◆ ◆

½ cup sugar
⅓ cup unsweetened cocoa powder
3 tablespoons (packed) cornstarch
1 teaspoon all purpose flour
 Pinch of salt
2 cups cold low-fat (1%) milk
1 teaspoon unsalted butter
1 teaspoon vanilla extract
⅛ teaspoon almond extract

Mix first 5 ingredients in heavy medium saucepan. Add 1 cup milk and whisk to dissolve cornstarch. Whisk in remaining milk. Whisk mixture over medium heat until thickened and beginning to simmer, about 5 minutes. Simmer 1 minute, stirring constantly. Remove from heat. Stir in butter and vanilla and almond extracts.

Divide pudding among 4 custard cups. Chill until cold, about 2 hours. *(Can be made 1 day ahead. Cover; keep chilled.)*

4 SERVINGS

COOKING WITH COCOA

Cocoa powder is a great way to have your chocolate and eat it, too—minus any guilt. It adds a deep, rich taste to baked goods without adding much fat. In fact, most cocoa powders have no more than seven grams of fat per ounce, with the most common supermarket brands checking in at about three grams.

The two unsweetened cocoa powders used for baking are Dutch-process and all-purpose or natural cocoa. Treated with alkali to neutralize its natural acidity, the Dutch-process kind is imported from Europe. It has a deep dark color. The other all-purpose cocoa, which is more common in supermarkets, is lighter in color than its European counterpart, which is not to say that its taste is weaker. In fact, chocolate experts tend to disagree over which cocoa packs the biggest chocolate punch. Some say that Dutch-process is less bitter, enabling a richer chocolate flavor to come through. Others argue that because the all-purpose unsweetened cocoa has not been treated, it has a more intense flavor. Both kinds, which are interchangeable in recipes, provide great chocolate taste while keeping fat down.

◆ ◆ ◆

Chocolate-Whiskey Truffle Soufflés with Caramel Sauce

◆ ◆ ◆

TRUFFLES

¾   cup whipping cream
10   ounces bittersweet (not unsweetened) or
     semisweet chocolate, chopped
¼   cup whiskey

SAUCE

1½   cups whipping cream
1   vanilla bean, split lengthwise
¾   cup sugar
¼   cup water

SOUFFLES

4   large eggs, separated
¼   cup plus 2 tablespoons sugar
1½   tablespoons cornstarch
1   tablespoon unsweetened cocoa powder
⅔   cup milk (do not use low-fat or nonfat)
4   ounces bittersweet (not unsweetened) or semisweet chocolate,
     finely chopped
1   tablespoon unsalted butter
½   vanilla bean, split lengthwise
¼   cup whiskey

     Additional sugar (for soufflé dishes)

     Powdered sugar

FOR TRUFFLES: Bring cream to boil in heavy medium saucepan. Remove from heat. Add chocolate; whisk until chocolate melts and mixture is smooth. Mix in whiskey. Refrigerate until chocolate truffle mixture is cold and firm, at least 2 hours.

Drop truffle mixture by tablespoonfuls onto waxed paper. Line baking sheet with foil. Roll each chocolate drop between palms into ball (if truffle sticks to hands, dust hands with unsweetened cocoa powder); place on baking sheet. Freeze until hard, about 1 hour; then cover. *(Can be made 1 week ahead. Keep frozen.)*

After dropping tablespoonfuls of the chilled truffle mixture onto waxed paper, roll them into smooth rounds; work quickly to prevent the chocolate truffles from softening.

To keep the egg yolks from curdling, whisk the hot chocolate mixture into the yolks gradually.

As the soufflé base cooks double-boiler style over simmering water, the yolks will cause it to thicken to a dense pudding consistency.

FOR SAUCE: Place cream in small bowl. Scrape seeds from vanilla bean. Mix seeds and bean into cream. Stir sugar and water in heavy medium saucepan over low heat until sugar dissolves. Increase heat; boil without stirring until syrup turns deep amber color, brushing down sides of pan with wet pastry brush and swirling pan occasionally, about 10 minutes. Remove from heat; add cream (mixture will bubble vigorously). Return pan to low heat; stir until caramel is smooth. Boil until color deepens and caramel thickens, stirring occasionally, about 2 minutes. Strain caramel into small bowl. Chill. *(Can be made 1 week ahead. Cover; keep chilled.)*

FOR SOUFFLES: Whisk yolks to blend in medium bowl; set aside. Whisk ¼ cup sugar, cornstarch and cocoa in medium stainless steel bowl until no cornstarch lumps remain. Whisk in milk. Add chocolate and butter. Scrape in seeds from vanilla bean; add bean. Place bowl with chocolate mixture over saucepan of simmering water (do not allow bottom of bowl to touch water). Whisk until mixture is smooth, about 2 minutes. Remove from over water. Gradually whisk some of hot chocolate mixture into yolks. Whisk yolk mixture back into bowl with chocolate mixture. Place over simmering water. Whisk until smooth and thickened to pudding consistency, about 4 minutes. Remove from over water. Gradually mix in whiskey. Remove bean; cool to lukewarm.

Preheat oven to 450°F. Butter eight ⅔- to ¾-cup soufflé dishes or custard cups; dust with sugar. Arrange dishes on baking sheet. Place 1 truffle in each dish. Using electric mixer, beat whites in medium bowl until soft peaks form. Gradually add 2 tablespoons sugar, beating until stiff but not dry. Fold whites into lukewarm soufflé base in 2 additions. Divide soufflé mixture among prepared dishes, filling almost to top. *(Can be prepared 1 week ahead. Cover dishes with foil and freeze. Uncover but do not thaw before baking.)*

Place soufflés on baking sheet in oven; reduce temperature to 400°F. Bake until puffed and dry-looking on top, about 17 minutes for unfrozen or 22 minutes for frozen. Transfer dishes to plates. Sift powdered sugar over. Serve, passing cold caramel sauce separately.

MAKES 8

For best results, beat the egg whites just until stiff and glossy, but not dry. The air beaten into the whites helps the soufflés rise.

The egg whites are folded into the soufflé base in two batches. The first addition loosens and lightens the heavy and slightly warm base.

After placing the truffles in the individual soufflé dishes, divide the soufflé batter among the dishes, filling them almost to the top.

Praline-Chocolate Crème Brûlée

◆ ◆ ◆

Crunchy praline is paired with rich chocolate custard in this elegant crème brûlée. Begin making this a day ahead because it needs to set up in the refrigerator overnight. There will be some praline leftover, which would make a terrific topping for ice cream.

◆ ◆ ◆

Nonstick vegetable oil spray
⅓   cup plus 2 tablespoons hazelnuts, toasted, finely chopped
1½ cups plus 3 tablespoons sugar
⅓   cup water

1¼ cups whipping cream
⅓   cup half and half
3   ounces bittersweet (not unsweetened) or semisweet chocolate, chopped
4   large egg yolks

Preheat oven to 350°F. Spray rimmed baking sheet with vegetable oil spray; sprinkle ⅓ cup nuts in center. Stir 1½ cups sugar and water in heavy small saucepan over medium-low heat until sugar dissolves. Increase heat and boil without stirring until syrup turns medium amber, occasionally swirling pan and brushing down sides of pan with pastry brush dipped into water. Working quickly, pour enough caramel into each of four ¾-cup soufflé dishes or custard cups to reach depth of ¼ inch. Sprinkle 1 teaspoon nuts onto caramel in each dish. Pour remaining caramel over nuts on baking sheet. Let stand until caramel cools completely.

Heat cream and half and half in medium saucepan over medium heat until beginning to simmer. Remove from heat. Add chocolate and whisk until melted and smooth. Beat yolks and remaining 3 tablespoons sugar in medium bowl to blend. Gradually whisk in warm chocolate mixture. Divide custard among prepared dishes. Place dishes in 13 x 9 x 2-inch baking pan. Pour enough hot water into pan to reach halfway up sides of dishes.

Bake custards until barely set in center, about 25 minutes. Remove pan with custards from oven; let custards stand in water bath 10 minutes. Transfer custards to rack and cool completely. Cover and refrigerate custards overnight.

Meanwhile, break cooled praline into small pieces. Transfer to processor and chop finely. *(Can be prepared 1 day ahead. Store all praline in airtight container at room temperature.)*

Preheat broiler. Sprinkle 2 teaspoons chopped praline over each custard. (Reserve remaining praline for another use.) Place custards on small baking sheet. Broil until praline begins to melt and bubble, about 1 minute. Refrigerate custards until praline hardens, at least 1 hour and up to 8 hours.

4 SERVINGS

Chocolate-Espresso Pots de Crème

◆ ◆ ◆

2½ cups chilled whipping cream
1   tablespoon plus 1 teaspoon instant espresso powder
5   ounces bittersweet (not unsweetened) or
     semisweet chocolate, finely chopped

6   large egg yolks, room temperature
2   tablespoons sugar
1   teaspoon vanilla extract
     Pinch of salt

     Chocolate coffee bean candies*

Position rack in center of oven and preheat to 325°F. Combine 2 cups cream and espresso powder in heavy medium saucepan. Bring to simmer, whisking to dissolve espresso powder. Remove from heat. Add chocolate; whisk until smooth.

Whisk egg yolks, sugar, vanilla and salt in large bowl until well blended. Gradually whisk in chocolate mixture. Strain custard.

Place six ¾-cup soufflé dishes or custard cups in large roasting pan. Divide custard equally among dishes. Pour enough hot water into pan to come halfway up sides of dishes. Cover pan with foil. Bake until custard is just set around edges but still soft in center, about 25 minutes. Remove dishes from water and cool. Cover and chill at least 2 hours. *(Can be prepared 1 day ahead. Keep chilled.)*

Beat remaining ½ cup cream in large bowl until peaks form. Spoon whipped cream into pastry bag fitted with large star tip. Pipe 1 large rosette in center of each custard. Garnish with chocolate coffee bean candies and serve chilled.

*Chocolate coffee bean candies are available at candy shops, specialty foods stores and some supermarkets.

6 SERVINGS

◆ ◆ ◆

Here, the French version of chocolate pudding (pictured on page 168) gets accented with espresso powder for a simple but seductive dessert. Chocolate-covered coffee beans add the finishing touch.

◆ ◆ ◆

ABOUT PUFF PASTRY

Puff pastry, delicate yet rich-tasting, is a classic recipe in the French tradition. It is used in a variety of sweets and savories: mille-feuilles, a French pastry (sometimes called a Napoleon) made with layers of puff pastry and sweetened whipped cream; *palmiers*, crisp palm-leaf-shaped pastries; fruit-filled turnovers; beef Wellington, which is wrapped in puff pastry; and *pâté en croûte*, pâté in puff pastry. It also makes a terrific tart shell or top crust for chicken pot pie.

Notoriously difficult to make, puff pastry requires a complex rolling and folding process of the dough with butter. The dough is wrapped around the butter and then rolled into a long rectangle, folded into thirds and turned one-quarter rotation. The rolling, folding and turning is repeated again, followed by 30 minutes of chilling. This process is usually repeated two to three more times. When baked, the moisture from the water in the dough creates steam, which causes the pastry to "puff" and separate into hundreds of crisp, flaky layers.

The good news is that prepared puff pastry dough is available in supermarkets nationwide, making it easier than ever to prepare your favorite puff pastry recipes at home.

◆ ◆ ◆

White Chocolate and Summer Berry Napoleons

◆ ◆ ◆

12 ounces good-quality white chocolate (such as Lindt or Baker's), chopped
½ cup milk (do not use low-fat or nonfat)

2½ cups chilled whipping cream
1 teaspoon vanilla extract

1 17¼-ounce package frozen puff pastry (2 sheets), thawed

2 5- to 6-ounce baskets blackberries
2 8½-ounce baskets strawberries, hulled, halved
2 6-ounce baskets blueberries
2 6-ounce baskets raspberries
Powdered sugar

Stir white chocolate in large bowl set over saucepan of barely simmering water until melted and smooth. Remove chocolate from heat. Bring milk to simmer in heavy medium saucepan. Whisk milk into chocolate. Let chocolate mixture cool until just beginning to thicken, stirring occasionally, about 1 hour.

Using electric mixer, beat cream and vanilla in another large bowl until medium-firm peaks form. Fold whipped cream into chocolate mixture in 3 additions. Cover and refrigerate.

Preheat oven to 400°F. Line 17¼ x 11½ x 1-inch baking sheet with parchment paper. Roll out 1 pastry sheet on lightly floured surface to 15 x 12-inch rectangle. Cut crosswise into three 12 x 5-inch rectangles. Repeat rolling and cutting with remaining pastry sheet to make six 12 x 5-inch pastry rectangles total. Transfer 2 pastry rectangles to prepared baking sheet, spacing evenly. Cover remaining pastry rectangles and chill.

Pierce pastry rectangles on baking sheet all over with fork. Top with second piece of parchment. Place another 17¼ x 11½ x 1-inch baking sheet atop parchment to weigh down pastry rectangles as they cook. Bake pastries until edges and bottoms are golden, about 10 minutes. Remove baking sheet and parchment paper from atop pastries. Turn pastries over. Continue baking uncovered until bottoms are golden, about 5 minutes longer. Transfer pastries to rack; cool. Repeat piercing and baking with remaining 4 pastry rectangles in 2 more batches. *(White chocolate cream and pastry rectangles can be prepared 1 day ahead. Keep cream refrigerated. Store pastry rectangles airtight at room temperature.)*

Place 1 pastry rectangle on work surface. Spread 1½ cups of chocolate cream over pastry. Gently toss all berries in large bowl. Arrange ¼ of berries in single layer over chocolate cream. Place second pastry rectangle atop berries. Spread 1½ cups of chocolate cream atop second pastry rectangle. Top with ¼ of berries. Top with third pastry rectangle. Repeat with remaining 3 pastry rectangles, chocolate cream and berries to form second napoleon. *(Can be made 4 hours ahead. Refrigerate.)* Using serrated knife, cut each pastry crosswise into 10 pieces. Sprinkle powdered sugar over each.

20 SERVINGS

Vanilla Rice Pudding with Dried Cherries

◆ ◆ ◆

4	cups plus 1 tablespoon milk (do not use low-fat or nonfat)
½	cup medium-grain white rice
½	cup sugar
½	teaspoon ground cinnamon
¼	teaspoon salt
1½	teaspoons cornstarch
3	large eggs
½	cup dried tart cherries or cranberries
2	teaspoons vanilla extract
1	teaspoon fresh lemon juice

Combine 4 cups milk, rice, sugar, cinnamon and salt in heavy large saucepan. Bring to boil over medium-high heat, stirring frequently. Reduce heat to medium and simmer until rice is very tender, stirring occasionally, about 25 minutes.

Whisk cornstarch and 1 tablespoon milk in large bowl to blend. Add eggs; whisk to blend. Whisk in hot rice mixture. Return to saucepan. Add cherries; stir over low heat just until mixture comes to boil. Mix in vanilla and lemon juice. Serve warm or pour pudding into buttered medium bowl. Press plastic wrap onto surface. Refrigerate until cold, at least 8 hours or overnight. Spoon vanilla rice pudding into bowls and serve.

6 SERVINGS

◆ ◆ ◆

This equally good served warm or cold. If you prefer rice pudding cold, begin preparing the dessert well ahead so that it has time to chill.

◆ ◆ ◆

◆ FROZEN DESSERTS ◆

Lemon-Lime Ring with Mixed Berries and Mango

◆ ◆ ◆

◆ ◆ ◆

This luscious recipe starts with a parfait, a French word that means "perfect." Parfaits are surprisingly easy to prepare and taste just like ice cream, only you don't need an ice cream machine. They are basically a frozen mousse made of egg yolks cooked with sugar, butter and flavorings (lemon and lime here), then lightened with whipped cream.

◆ ◆ ◆

MOUSSE

1½	cups sugar
8	large egg yolks
⅓	cup fresh lemon juice
⅓	cup fresh lime juice
5	tablespoons unsalted butter
2	teaspoons grated lemon peel
2	cups chilled whipping cream

FRUIT

1	12-ounce basket strawberries, hulled, quartered
1	tablespoon sugar
2	mangoes, peeled, pitted, cubed
1	6-ounce basket raspberries
1	6-ounce basket blackberries or boysenberries
1	6-ounce basket blueberries

Fresh lime- and lemon-peel twists
Fresh mint sprigs

FOR MOUSSE: Line 12-cup ring mold with plastic wrap; allow plastic to overhang edges by 3 inches. Whisk first 6 ingredients in large metal bowl to blend. Set over saucepan of simmering water (do not allow bowl to touch water); whisk until candy thermometer registers 180°F, about 7 minutes. Remove from over water. Using electric mixer, beat mixture until cool and thick, about 8 minutes.

Beat cream in another large bowl until stiff peaks form. Fold cream into egg mixture. Spoon into mold; smooth top. Cover and freeze overnight. *(Can be prepared 1 week ahead. Keep frozen.)*

FOR FRUIT: Toss strawberries with sugar in large bowl. Let stand 20 minutes. Add cubed mangoes, raspberries, blackberries and blueberries and toss to coat.

Turn frozen mousse out onto platter. Peel off plastic. Smooth top and sides with metal icing spatula. Mound some fruit in center of mousse. Garnish with lime- and lemon-peel twists and mint. Serve, passing remaining fruit separately.

12 SERVINGS

Granitas are made by scraping the surface of a frozen sweetened liquid to form icy flakes. A big plus to this refreshing Italian ice is that it is prepared without an ice cream maker. (Here, a bowl of Raspberry Granita is shown with the Pine Nut Crescents from page 217.)

◆ ◆ ◆

Raspberry Granita

◆ ◆ ◆

1   cup water

¾   cup plus 2 tablespoons sugar

3   cups fresh raspberries (about 16 ounces)

1   tablespoon fresh lemon juice

Fresh raspberries

Combine water and sugar in medium saucepan. Stir over medium heat until sugar dissolves. Bring to boil. Remove from heat. Refrigerate syrup until cold.

Meanwhile, mash 3 cups raspberries in medium bowl. Stir in lemon juice. Mix in sugar syrup. Pour mixture through strainer, pressing on solids to extract as much liquid as possible. Pour mixture into shallow baking dish. Freeze granita until almost firm, stirring frequently, approximately 2 hours.

Continue freezing granita until firm (do not stir), at least 3 hours or overnight. *(Can be made 3 days ahead. Cover; keep frozen.)*

Using fork, scrape surface of granita to form crystals. Scoop crystals into glasses. Garnish with raspberries.

6 SERVINGS

Plum Granita with Mixed Fruit

◆ ◆ ◆

¾   cup water

½   cup sugar

2   whole allspice

1   cinnamon stick

½   vanilla bean, split lengthwise

1½   pounds plums, preferably red-fleshed (about 7 large), pitted, cut into ¾-inch pieces

1   peach, pitted, thinly sliced

1   nectarine, pitted, thinly sliced

1   plum, pitted, thinly sliced

Combine water, sugar, allspice and cinnamon in heavy small saucepan. Scrape in seeds from vanilla bean; add bean. Bring to boil, stirring until sugar dissolves. Reduce heat and simmer until liquid is reduced to ¾ cup, about 2 minutes. Cool syrup completely.

Puree 1½ pounds plums in processor. Press enough puree through sieve to measure 1½ cups. Strain syrup into puree and blend well. Transfer mixture to 9 x 5 x 3-inch glass loaf dish. Freeze plum mixture until flaky crystals form, stirring every 30 minutes, about 4 hours. *(Can be made 1 week ahead. Cover; keep frozen.)*

Spoon granita into 4 glass goblets. Top with peach, nectarine and plum slices and serve immediately.

4 SERVINGS

Pistachio Gelato

◆ ◆ ◆

¾   cup unsalted shelled pistachios (about 3¾ ounces)

¾   cup sugar

2   cups milk (do not use low-fat or nonfat)

1   teaspoon almond extract

5   large egg yolks

2   drops green food coloring

     Chopped unsalted pistachios

Finely grind ¾ cup pistachios and ¼ cup sugar in processor. Combine pistachio mixture, milk and almond extract in heavy medium saucepan. Bring to boil. Whisk yolks and ½ cup sugar in large bowl to blend. Gradually whisk milk mixture into yolk mixture. Return mixture to saucepan. Stir over medium-low heat until custard thickens slightly and leaves path on back of spoon when finger is drawn across, about 8 minutes (do not boil). Remove from heat. Whisk in food coloring. Chill custard until cold, about 3 hours.

Process custard in ice cream maker according to manufacturer's instructions. Transfer to covered container and freeze. *(Can be prepared 1 week ahead. Keep frozen.)* Scoop gelato into glasses or bowls. Garnish with chopped pistachios.

6 SERVINGS

Gelato is made from whole milk, egg yolks, sugar and natural flavoring. This version (shown here with the Cornmeal Diamonds from page 218) calls for pistachio nuts. Softer in texture and more intense in taste and color than typical ice cream, gelato is one of Italy's great culinary creations.

◆ ◆ ◆

Chocolate and Almond Spumoni

◆ ◆ ◆

4   large egg yolks
¾   cup sugar
2   tablespoons cornstarch
2½ cups milk (do not use low-fat or nonfat)
3   ounces semisweet chocolate, chopped
1   cup blanched slivered almonds, toasted, chopped (about 4 ounces)

1½ cups chilled whipping cream
1   tablespoon powdered sugar

Whisk yolks, ¾ cup sugar and cornstarch in heavy medium saucepan to blend. Bring milk to simmer in heavy small saucepan. Gradually whisk hot milk into yolk mixture. Stir over medium heat until custard thickens and boils and leaves path on back of spoon when finger is drawn across, about 2 minutes. Remove from heat. Add chopped chocolate and whisk until melted. Stir in chopped almonds. Transfer custard to large bowl. Freeze until cold but not firm, stirring occasionally, about 45 minutes.

Line 9 x 5 x 2½-inch loaf pan with plastic, leaving overhang. Beat chilled whipping cream and powdered sugar in large bowl until medium-firm peaks form. Fold cream into custard. Transfer to pan. Fold plastic over. Cover with foil; freeze until firm, at least 8 hours. *(Can be prepared 3 days ahead.)*

Remove foil from pan. Let spumoni stand 30 minutes. Invert onto platter. Remove plastic. Cut into slices and serve.

10 TO 12 SERVINGS

Here's an elegant frozen dessert of Neapolitan origin that manages to be rich and light at the same time. Its airy texture is reflected in its lyrical name, which comes from the Italian word for foam, *spuma.*

◆ ◆ ◆

Coffee Ice Cream Sundaes with Pine Nut-Caramel Sauce

◆ ◆ ◆

1   cup sugar
3   tablespoons water
1   cup whipping cream
2   tablespoons unsalted butter
1   cup pine nuts, toasted

Coffee ice cream

Stir sugar and water in heavy medium saucepan over medium heat until sugar dissolves. Increase heat; boil without stirring until syrup turns deep amber, occasionally brushing down sides with wet pastry brush and swirling pan, about 6 minutes. Remove from heat. Slowly mix in cream (sauce will bubble vigorously). Add butter; stir over medium-low heat until smooth. Add nuts. Cool slightly. *(Can be made 1 day ahead. Cover; chill. Before continuing, stir over medium heat until warm.)*

Spoon ice cream into bowls. Spoon warm sauce over.

8 SERVINGS

Cantaloupe Sorbet

◆ ◆ ◆

⅔   cup sugar
½   cup water

3   cups 1-inch pieces peeled seeded cantaloupe (about ½ cantaloupe)

Combine sugar and water in medium saucepan. Stir over medium heat until sugar dissolves. Bring to boil. Transfer sugar syrup to 11 x 7 x 2-inch glass dish; chill until cold, about 2 hours.

Puree cantaloupe in blender until smooth. Add to sugar syrup in dish and stir until well blended. Freeze until almost firm, stirring occasionally, at least 3 hours or overnight.

Transfer cantaloupe mixture to large bowl. Using electric mixer, beat until fluffy. Return to freezer and freeze until firm (do not stir), at least 3 hours or overnight. *(Sorbet can be prepared 3 days ahead. Cover and keep frozen.)*

6 SERVINGS

Like a French sorbet, this Italian recipe is made from sugar, water and fruit pulp. Unlike a French sorbet, it is frozen without being processed in an ice cream maker. (The Walnut-Raisin Cookies from page 219 complete the dessert.)

◆ ◆ ◆

Brownie Sundaes with Banana Chips

◆ ◆ ◆

SAUCE

¾   cup whipping cream

9   ounces semisweet chocolate, chopped

BROWNIES

16 ounces semisweet chocolate, chopped

1   cup (2 sticks) unsalted butter

1¼ cups sugar

6   large eggs, separated

    Powdered sugar

2   quarts vanilla ice cream

½   cup dried banana chips

FOR SAUCE: Bring cream to simmer in medium saucepan. Remove from heat. Add chocolate; stir until smooth. *(Can be prepared 1 day ahead. Cover; chill. Rewarm over low heat.)*

FOR BROWNIES: Preheat oven to 350°F. Butter 13 x 9-inch metal baking pan. Line bottom with parchment paper. Butter paper; dust sides of pan and paper with flour. Tap out excess. Melt chocolate and butter in heavy large saucepan over low heat, stirring until smooth. Cool to room temperature.

Using electric mixer, beat ½ cup sugar and yolks in large bowl until thick, about 4 minutes. Stir in chocolate mixture. Using electric mixer fitted with clean dry beaters, beat egg whites in another large bowl until soft peaks form. Gradually beat in ¾ cup sugar. Continue beating until stiff peaks form. Using rubber spatula, gently fold whites into chocolate mixture in 3 additions.

Pour batter into prepared pan. Bake until brownie cracks around edges and tester inserted into center comes out with moist crumbs attached, about 35 minutes. Cool on rack. *(Can be made 1 day ahead. Wrap tightly; store at room temperature.)*

Run knife around sides of brownie. Place baking sheet atop pan; invert brownie onto baking sheet. Remove pan. Peel off parchment. Invert brownie onto another baking sheet. Cut into 12 pieces.

Place 1 brownie in center of each plate. Sprinkle with sugar. Top with ice cream. Spoon sauce over. Sprinkle with banana chips.

12 SERVINGS

◆ ◆ ◆

The brownie in these sundaes is really more like a flourless chocolate cake. It puffs as it bakes, and then falls and cracks as it cools.

◆ ◆ ◆

Pineapple-Rum Ice Cream

◆ ◆ ◆

3   cups whipping cream
1   cup milk (do not use low-fat or nonfat)
1   vanilla bean, split lengthwise
2¼ cups sugar
¾   cup dark rum
10 large egg yolks
½   cup pineapple juice

2   cups finely chopped fresh pineapple

Combine cream and milk in heavy large saucepan. Scrape in seeds from vanilla bean; add bean. Bring to simmer. Remove from heat. Mix in ¾ cup sugar and ¼ cup rum. Whisk yolks and ¾ cup sugar in large bowl until beginning to thicken. Whisk in pineapple juice, then hot cream mixture. Return to saucepan. Stir over medium-low heat until custard thickens and leaves path on back of spoon when finger is drawn across, about 10 minutes (do not boil). Strain mixture into large bowl. Chill until cold, about 2 hours.

Meanwhile, mix ¾ cup sugar, ½ cup rum and chopped pineapple in medium bowl. Let stand 1 hour. Bring to boil. Reduce heat and simmer 3 minutes, stirring occasionally. Drain pineapple. Cool.

Process custard in ice cream maker until beginning to thicken. Add pineapple; process until semi-firm. Transfer to container; cover and freeze until firm, about 3 hours. *(Can be made 4 days ahead.)*

MAKES ABOUT 7 CUPS

Chopped fresh pineapple is a welcome addition to this tropical-tasting ice cream. It's great served with purchased caramel sauce.

Pineapple-Coconut Tuiles with Mascarpone Cream

◆ ◆ ◆

COCONUT TUILES

Nonstick vegetable oil spray

2 cups unsweetened shredded coconut* (about 5 ounces)

¼ cup all purpose flour

1¼ cups sugar

2 tablespoons plus 1 teaspoon unsalted butter, room temperature

¾ cup egg whites (about 6 large)

PINEAPPLE SYRUP

3 cups canned unsweetened pineapple juice

½ cup sugar

7 cardamom pods, cut in half

1 teaspoon black peppercorns

2 whole cloves

1 cinnamon stick

½ jalapeño chili with seeds

1 large pineapple, peeled, cored, cut into 12 rounds (each about ⅓ inch thick)

MASCARPONE CREAM

12 ounces mascarpone cheese** (about 1 cup plus 2 tablespoons)

1¼ cups chilled whipping cream

¼ cup sugar

1 tablespoon dark rum

1 12-ounce basket strawberries, hulled, sliced

FOR COCONUT TUILES: Preheat oven to 300°F. Spray large nonstick baking sheet with vegetable oil spray. Mix coconut and flour in small bowl. Using electric mixer, beat sugar and butter in large bowl until blended. Gradually add egg whites and beat until mixture thickens slightly. Stir in coconut mixture.

Form 2 tuiles by spooning 1 very generous tablespoonful batter for each tuile onto prepared baking sheet, spacing 4 inches apart. Using small metal spatula or back of spoon, spread batter to thin 3- to 3½-inch rounds. Bake until tuiles are golden, about 22 minutes. Working quickly and using metal spatula, transfer tuiles to

The coconut tuiles (cookies) that go into this layered dessert are delicate, so the recipe provides for quite a few extras to allow for breakage. Tuiles are also terrific with ice cream. The syrup gets an interesting (and delicious) kick from nontraditional dessert ingredients like black peppercorns and a jalapeño chili.

◆ ◆ ◆

racks. Return baking sheet to oven briefly if tuiles harden and stick slightly to sheet. Working in batches, repeat with remaining batter, spraying baking sheet before each batch. Cool tuiles completely.

FOR PINEAPPLE SYRUP: Boil first 7 ingredients in heavy large pot until liquid is reduced to 2½ cups, about 4 minutes. Arrange pineapple rounds in layers in pot. Reduce heat to medium; cover and cook until pineapple is tender and translucent, turning rounds occasionally, about 20 minutes. Using slotted spoon, transfer pineapple rounds to large baking sheet. Cool. Strain pineapple cooking liquid; return to same pot. Boil until syrup is reduced to ½ cup, about 5 minutes. Transfer to bowl and cool. *(Tuiles, pineapple and syrup can be prepared 1 day ahead. Store tuiles in airtight container. Cover and refrigerate pineapple and syrup separately. Bring to room temperature before assembling dessert.)*

FOR MASCARPONE CREAM: Beat mascarpone, cream and sugar in large bowl until firm peaks form. Beat in rum.

Place 1 tuile on each of 6 plates. Place 1 pineapple round atop each. Spread 3 tablespoons mascarpone cream atop pineapple round. Top with another tuile, 3 tablespoons mascarpone cream, then 1 pineapple round. Spoon remaining mascarpone cream into pastry bag fitted with medium star tip. Pipe rosettes in center of pineapple rounds. Drizzle pineapple syrup around tuiles. Surround with strawberry slices and serve.

*Unsweetened coconut is available at natural foods stores.

**Available at Italian markets and most supermarkets.

MAKES 6

Fudgy Chocolate-Raspberry Bars

◆ ◆ ◆

In this recipe, dense chocolate cake is topped with a glaze made from raspberry jam and chocolate—fresh berries are the finishing touch. The dessert is elegant, whether served in the dining room or at a picnic. Prepare the bars a day ahead.

◆ ◆ ◆

CAKE

10   ounces bittersweet (not unsweetened) or semisweet chocolate, chopped

¾   cup (1½ sticks) unsalted butter, cut into small pieces

⅓   cup seedless raspberry jam

1   cup sugar

5   large eggs

⅓   cup all purpose flour

1   teaspoon baking powder

GLAZE

¼   cup whipping cream

¼   cup seedless raspberry jam

6   ounces bittersweet (not unsweetened) or semisweet chocolate, chopped

2   6-ounce baskets fresh raspberries

FOR CAKE: Preheat oven to 350°F. Line 9 x 9 x 2-inch baking pan with foil. Butter foil; dust with flour. Stir chocolate and butter in heavy medium saucepan over low heat until melted and smooth. Add jam and whisk until melted. Cool slightly.

Using electric mixer, beat sugar and eggs in large bowl until mixture thickens, about 6 minutes. Sift flour and baking powder over egg mixture and fold in. Gradually fold in chocolate mixture.

Pour batter into pan. Bake until top of cake is slightly crusty, begins to crack and tester inserted into center comes out with moist crumbs attached, about 45 minutes. Cool 5 minutes. Gently press down any raised edges of cake to even. Cool in pan. Invert cake onto platter. Peel off foil. Trim ½ inch off each edge of cake.

FOR GLAZE: Stir cream and jam in heavy small saucepan over medium heat until jam melts; bring to boil. Remove from heat. Add chocolate and stir until melted. Let stand until glaze is cool but still spreadable, about 15 minutes.

Spread glaze over top of cake. Immediately arrange berries atop glaze. Chill until glaze sets, about 10 minutes. *(Can be made 1 day ahead. Cover and keep refrigerated.)*

Cut cake into 12 even pieces and then serve.

12 SERVINGS

◆ INDEX ◆

Page numbers in *italics* indicate color photographs.

Acknowledgments

◆ ◆ ◆

The following people contributed the recipes included in this book: Colin Ambrose; Noel Ampel, Aquavit, New York, New York; John Ash; Carolyn Baker; Mary Barber; Karen Barker; Melanie Barnard; Nancy Verde Barr; Paul Bartolotta; Maria Battaglia; Octavio Becerra; Anna Bruni Benson; Cherryl and Tom Berthiaume; Lula Bertran; Jan Birnbaum; Lena Cederham Birnbaum; Carole Bloom; Frank Cepero; Alex Castro; Shelley Cooper; Agathe Corby; Sara Corpening; Lane Crowther; Nancy Currey; Da Diretto, Capitignano, Italy; David Paul's Lahaina Grill, Lahaina, Maui, Hawaii; Janet Hazen De Jesus; Lorenza de' Medici; Lisa Digrandi; Brooke Dojny; Kathy and Robert Du Grenier; Mark Ellman; Bruno Feldeisen; Barbara Pool Fenzl; Claudia Fleming; Jim Fobel; Millie Pozzo Froeb; Margaret and Stephen Gadient; Marcella Giamundo; Gordon Biersch, Honolulu, Oahu, Hawaii; Sophie Grigson; Kathy Gunst; Ken Haedrich; Clifford Harrison; Inn of the Anasazi, Santa Fe, New Mexico; Steve Johnson; Erasmo "Razz" Kamnitzer; Karen Kaplan; Loretta Keller; Jeanne Thiel Kelley; Kristine Kidd; Jennifer Kirkgaard; Landgasthof Ruedihus, Kandersteg, Switzerland; The Lodge at Koele, Lanai, Hawaii; Michael McLaughlin; Miraval, Catalina, Arizona; Jinx and Jefferson Morgan; Selma Brown Morrow; Gina and Rich Mortillaro; Kristen and Andrew Murray; Antonella Nonino; Rochelle Palermo; Nora Pouillon; Anne Quatrano; Red Light, Chicago, Illinois; Rhett's, Nashville, Tennessee; Mimi Rippee; Claudia Roden; Douglas Rodriguez; Betty Rosbottom; Nicole Routhier; Arun Sampanthavivat; Marie Simmons; Marcello Spadone; Sarah Tenaglia; Mary Jo Thoresen; Rick Tramonto; Karen and Tom Uhlmann; Norman Van Aken; Chris Watson; Joanne Weir; Lisa A. Wilson; Clifford A. Wright; Terri Pischoff Wuerthner.

The following people contributed the photographs included in this book: Jack Andersen; Maryellen Baker; Noel Barnhurst; David Bishop; Antoine Bootz; Cynthia Brown; Dave Carlin; Wendy Carlson; Steve Cohen; Wyatt Counts; Julie Dennis; Greg Gillis; Charles Imstepf; John Kelly; Hacob Khodaverdian; Eric L. Klein; Deborah Klesenski; Brian Leatart; Michael Luppino; Andrew Martin; Maura McEvoy; Gary Moss; Judd Pilossof; Stephanie Rausser; David Roth; France Ruffenach; Jeff Sarpa; Rick Szczechowski; Mark Thomas; Laurie Vogt; Louis Wallach; Elizabeth Watt.

Front jacket photo: Mark Thomas, Photographer; Dora Johenson, Food Stylist; Nancy Micklin, Prop Stylist.

Double-Nut Maple Bars

◆ ◆ ◆

CRUST

1¼ cups unbleached all purpose flour

⅓ cup sugar

Pinch of salt

6 tablespoons (¾ stick) chilled unsalted butter, cut into pieces

1 large egg yolk

1 tablespoon milk (do not use low-fat or nonfat milk)

FILLING

⅓ cup pure maple syrup

⅓ cup (packed) golden brown sugar

¼ cup whipping cream

2 tablespoons (¼ stick) unsalted butter

¾ cup pecans, toasted, coarsely chopped

¾ cup walnuts, toasted, coarsely chopped

½ teaspoon vanilla extract

FOR CRUST: Preheat oven to 350°F. Butter 8 x 8 x 2-inch metal baking pan. Combine flour, sugar and salt in processor and blend. Add butter and process until mixture resembles coarse meal. Combine egg yolk and milk in small bowl. Drizzle egg mixture into processor; process using on/off turns just until dough clumps together but is still dry. Transfer dough crumbs to prepared pan. Press crumbs onto bottom and halfway up sides of pan. Bake until crust is set and pale golden, about 25 minutes. Transfer crust to rack and cool.

FOR FILLING: Combine maple syrup, sugar, cream and butter in heavy medium saucepan. Bring mixture to boil. Boil 2 minutes. Remove from heat and stir in nuts and vanilla.

Pour filling over crust, spreading nuts evenly. Bake until filling bubbles all over, about 8 minutes. Transfer to rack and cool completely. Cut into bars and serve at room temperature. *(Can be prepared 1 day ahead. Store cookies between sheets of waxed paper in airtight container at room temperature.)*

MAKES 16

ABOUT MAPLE SYRUP

There are maple-flavored syrups and then there is *real* maple syrup. Pure maple syrup is made from the sap of maple trees—nothing else. All maple syrup is produced in North America, with Canada, Vermont and New York best known for producing superior maple syrup.

The maple trees are first tapped around late February. The sap is then collected for a period of four to six weeks. Because sap is 95 percent water, which has to be boiled off, it usually takes between 35 to 40 gallons of sap (and sometimes as much as 50) to make one gallon of maple syrup.

After the sap is reduced to a thick syrup, it is filtered and graded for quality. Using a grading system developed by the U.S. Department of agriculture, producers check the syrup for color and flavor. Of the different grades, Fancy is palest in color and has the most delicate flavor. With a dark amber color and a bold maple flavor, Grade B is the most robust variety and is typically used in cooking. All maple syrups, though, have the same consistency. Since pure maple syrup has no preservatives, it's best to refrigerate after opening.

◆ ◆ ◆

Lemon-Poppy Seed Sandwich Cookies

◆ ◆ ◆

Here are wonderful sugar cookies accented with the crunch of poppy seeds and a luscious lemon cream cheese filling. Assemble them shortly before serving to keep them crisp. If you like, you can skip the filling and serve the cookies on their own.

◆ ◆ ◆

COOKIES

2¾ cups all purpose flour
½   teaspoon salt
½   teaspoon baking powder
1   cup (2 sticks) unsalted butter, room temperature
1¼ cups sugar
1   large egg
2   tablespoons poppy seeds
2   teaspoons grated lemon peel
1   teaspoon vanilla extract
½   teaspoon lemon extract

FILLING

8   ounces cream cheese, room temperature
⅓   cup plus 1 tablespoon sugar
½   teaspoon lemon extract
¼   teaspoon vanilla extract

FOR COOKIES: Mix flour, salt and baking powder in medium bowl. Using electric mixer, beat butter in large bowl until light. Gradually beat in sugar. Beat in egg, then poppy seeds, lemon peel and extracts. Mix in dry ingredients in 3 additions. Gather dough into ball. Divide dough in half; flatten each half into disk. Wrap each dough disk in plastic; chill 2 hours.

Preheat oven to 325°F. Butter 2 large baking sheets. Roll out 1 dough disk on floured surface to ⅛-inch thickness. Using 2½-inch-diameter fluted cookie cutter, cut out cookies. Arrange cookies 1 inch apart on prepared baking sheets. Gather scraps; reroll and cut out more cookies. Chill cookies on baking sheets 15 minutes.

Bake cookies until edges just begin to color, about 18 minutes. Cool cookies on sheets 3 minutes. Transfer cookies to racks; cool completely. Repeat rolling, cutting and baking with remaining dough. (Can be made ahead. Store in airtight container at room temperature up to 2 weeks or freeze up to 1 month.)

FOR FILLING: Beat all ingredients in large bowl until light and fluffy. Spread 2 teaspoons filling over bottom of 1 cookie. Press second cookie, bottom side down, onto filling. Repeat with remaining cookies and filling. (Can be made 2 hours ahead. Cover; chill.)

MAKES ABOUT 27

Pine Nut Crescents

¾ cup blanched slivered almonds
1 cup sugar
2 tablespoons powdered sugar
2 tablespoons all purpose flour
   Pinch of salt
2 large egg whites

1¼ cups pine nuts (about 6 ounces)

Butter and lightly flour heavy large baking sheet. Finely grind almonds in processor. Add sugar, powdered sugar, flour and salt; process until well blended. Add egg whites; process until smooth dough forms (dough will be very sticky).

Spread pine nuts on floured surface. Using floured hands, form dough into 1-inch balls. Roll balls in pine nuts, pressing slightly to adhere. Form balls into crescents. Transfer to prepared baking sheet, spacing 1 inch apart. Let cookies stand at room temperature at least 1 hour and up to 2 hours before baking.

Preheat oven to 350°F. Bake cookies until golden brown, about 18 minutes. Transfer cookies to rack and cool completely. *(Can be prepared 2 days ahead. Store in airtight container.)*

MAKES ABOUT 18

These cookies have a wonderful chewy texture. The dough is very soft, so you will need to flour your fingers to shape it. But don't inadvertently use too much flour in the process, or the cookies will be tough.

Almond Meringues

◆ ◆ ◆

4 large egg whites
1½ cups powdered sugar
1½ cups blanched slivered almonds (about 6½ ounces)
3 tablespoons fresh lemon juice

Preheat oven to 300°F. Line 2 baking sheets with parchment paper. Butter parchment. Beat egg whites in large bowl until stiff peaks form. Gradually fold in powdered sugar, almonds and lemon juice (meringue will deflate and will no longer be stiff).

Drop meringue by level tablespoonfuls onto prepared baking sheets, spacing 2 inches apart. Bake until cookies are pale golden around edges, about 25 minutes. Cool completely on baking sheets. Using metal spatula, carefully remove cookies from parchment.

MAKES ABOUT 35

Ginger Shortbread Cookies

♦ ♦ ♦

2⅓ cups unbleached all purpose flour
¾ cup powdered sugar
2 teaspoons ground ginger
¼ teaspoon salt
¼ cup coarsely chopped crystallized ginger (about 1½ ounces)
1 tablespoon sugar

1 cup (2 sticks) unsalted butter, room temperature
2 teaspoons grated lemon peel
½ teaspoon lemon extract
½ teaspoon vanilla extract

Combine flour, ¾ cup powdered sugar, ground ginger and salt in medium bowl. Combine crystallized ginger and 1 tablespoon sugar on work surface; chop finely.

Using electric mixer, beat butter in large bowl until light. Add lemon peel and extracts. Beat in crystallized ginger mixture. Beat dry ingredients into butter mixture in 4 additions.

Transfer dough to floured work surface. Divide dough in half. Roll each half into 6-inch log. Shape each log into 2 x 1 x 6-inch-long rectangular log. Wrap in plastic and refrigerate 2 hours.

Preheat oven to 325°F. Lightly butter 2 large baking sheets. Cut each dough log into ⅓-inch-thick cookies. Transfer cookies to prepared baking sheets, spacing 1 inch apart (cookies will spread slightly during baking). Bake cookies until edges are pale golden, about 24 minutes. Cool cookies on baking sheets 3 minutes. Using metal spatula, transfer cookies to racks. Cool completely.

MAKES ABOUT 36

These delicate, buttery cookies are nice with a cup of tea or coffee. They can be made up to a week ahead (store them at room temperature in an airtight container).

♦ ♦ ♦

Cornmeal Diamonds

♦ ♦ ♦

2 cups unbleached all purpose flour
1½ cups yellow cornmeal
½ teaspoon salt
1 cup (2 sticks) unsalted butter, room temperature
¾ cup sugar
4 large egg yolks
2 tablespoons water
1½ teaspoons grated lemon peel

Preheat oven to 325°F. Butter and lightly flour 2 heavy large baking sheets. Sift flour, cornmeal and salt into large bowl. Beat butter and sugar in another large bowl until creamy. Beat in 3 yolks, 1 at a time, until well blended. Beat in dry ingredients in 3 additions. Mix in water and lemon peel; beat until smooth dough forms.

Turn dough out onto generously floured surface and knead until smooth, about 8 turns. Roll out dough to 6 x 8-inch rectangle about 1 inch thick. Cut rectangle into 1-inch diamond shapes. Transfer cookies to prepared baking sheets, spacing 2 inches apart.

Beat remaining yolk in bowl. Brush cookies with yolk. Bake until cookies are light golden, about 30 minutes. Transfer to racks; cool. *(Can be made 3 days ahead. Store in airtight container.)*

MAKES ABOUT 42

Walnut-Raisin Cookies

◆ ◆ ◆

2   cups raisins
2   cups all purpose flour
1   tablespoon baking powder
1½ cups sugar
1   cup (2 sticks) unsalted butter, room temperature
½   teaspoon vanilla extract
3   large eggs

3   cups walnuts

Place raisins in medium bowl. Pour enough boiling water over to cover; let stand 1 minute. Drain raisins well. Sift flour and baking powder into another medium bowl. Beat sugar and butter in large bowl until creamy. Beat in vanilla. Beat in 1 egg, then ⅓ of dry ingredients. Repeat with remaining eggs and dry ingredients in 2 batches. Stir in raisins (dough will be very soft). Refrigerate dough 1 hour to firm slightly.

Preheat oven to 375°F. Line 3 heavy large baking sheets with foil. Butter foil. Coarsely grind walnuts in processor. Mound ground walnuts on work surface. Working in batches, drop dough by scant tablespoonfuls onto walnuts (dough will be sticky). Using hands, roll dough in ground walnuts, coating completely and forming balls. Transfer to prepared baking sheets, spacing 2 inches apart.

Bake until cookies spread and are golden brown, about 14 minutes. Transfer to racks; cool completely.

MAKES ABOUT 60

◆ ◆ ◆

Called *nocelli* in Italian, these easy-to-make cookies are named after the Italian word for walnut, *noce*. (You can make them up to two days ahead; store in an airtight container.)

◆ ◆ ◆